FAITH AND CULTURE
IN THE
IRISH CONTEXT

Edited by Eoin G. Cassidy

VERITAS

First published 1996 by
Veritas Publications
7-8 Lower Abbey Street
Dublin 1

ISBN 1 85390 331 0

British Library Cataloguing
in Publication Data.
A catalogue record for
this book is available
from the British Library.

Cover design by Banahan Mc Manus Ltd, Dublin
Printed in the Republic of Ireland by Betaprint Ltd, Dublin

CONTENTS

INTRODUCTION

Eoin G. Cassidy

In treating of a theme such as that suggested by the title of this book the issue of perspective assumes a singular importance. This insight recently came home to me forcibly when I chanced upon a volume in the series entitled *A History of Irish Catholicism*, edited in the late 1960s by Patrick J. Corish. The volume in question was written by a well-known member of the Columban order, Joseph McGlade, and was entitled *The Missions: Africa and The Orient*.[1] The opening sentence reads as follows:

> The history of Catholicism in Ireland reveals two outstanding characteristics – pertinacity in the Faith and missionary zeal.[2]

The author proceeds to establish the latter thesis by drawing on a formidable array of statistics, showing the extent of the Irish missionary presence in Africa and the Orient in the course of the twentieth century. The facts are, indeed, impressive. In a short space of twenty-one years between 1916 and 1937, no fewer than five new Irish missionary institutes were established: the Columban Mission Society, the Kiltegan Fathers, the Medical Missionaries of Mary, the Holy Rosary Sisters and the Missionary Sisters of St Columban. By 1957 no less than ten per cent of all the priests and religious sisters on the African continent were of Irish birth – almost three thousand Irish religious missionaries in Africa alone.

Today, less than forty years later, these statistics seem almost incredible. It is not just that the missionary environment has changed in the intervening period, but the cultural climate in Ireland which sustained a truly massive missionary endeavour up until as recently as thirty years ago has altered almost beyond recognition. Nothing becomes dated so quickly as a thesis built upon the premise that the present is normative, and, from our perspective, at the close of the twentieth century, many of the assumptions in the 1950s about continued missionary growth seem so very questionable. If, with hindsight, we can see the folly of presuming an ever-increasing missionary vocations graph, so, likewise, we ourselves must be careful to recognise the folly of presuming to have attained that elusive vantage point commonly referred to as 'the objective standpoint'. The following examples may help to illustrate the importance of perspective.

There are those who suggest that the decrease in Irish religious missionary vocations is primarily attributable to a significant decline in the influence of religious beliefs and values on contemporary Irish society. What is not often adverted to is that this use of the term 'decrease in religious vocations' is a relative term. A decrease from what base – 1960? Thirty years previously there were fewer than two hundred Irish priests working in Africa and, thirty years previously again, probably fewer than two hundred Irish priests working as missionaries anywhere in the world. As the end of the twentieth century approaches, there are undoubtedly more Irish religious working as missionaries than there have been for over a thousand years, apart that is, from a brief period in the middle of this century. While not denying the recent evidence of a shift in values to what might loosely be called a more secularised society, the need for a sense of history is obvious.

The importance of perspective can also be seen when attempting to analyse the causes of change. For instance, there are few who would interpret the evidence of the recent decline in Irish religious missionary vocations without reference to the significant political and religious changes that have taken place in what used to be called the mission territories and to the growth in Irish lay missionary activity allied with the work of recently established Irish religious bodies such as Trócaire and Concern. Nevertheless, there is also the need to examine the cultural and socio-economic factors obtaining in Ireland in the first half of the twentieth century, with a view to ascertaining their influence on the dramatic increase in religious missionary vocations during this period. It is, to say the least, rash to presume that religious vocations can be understood simply as a barometer of religious beliefs and values shorn of any larger cultural considerations.

Finally, a sense of perspective is always valuable in countering the understandable tendency to treat a particular set of events as if they were unique to one particular geographical or historical location. For instance, when discussing changes in the Irish missionary profile, there can be the understandable tendency to lay emphasis on the changed cultural and religious environment in Ireland without taking into account the larger changes in culture which have affected and continue to affect the religious belief patterns of the so-called western world. In this context, it is interesting to note that in 1957 there were over two thousand French missionary priests working in Africa alone – and that from a country which currently has an acute shortage of priests. Notwithstanding the peculiarity of Irish history, the changes in Irish beliefs and values can only be understood if one is sensitive to the larger picture. Changing patterns of religious vocations are not unique to Ireland.

The type of perspective which is required to understand recent Irish missionary endeavour is also demanded in a more general way by the preoccupations of this present volume. The title *Faith and Culture in the Irish Context* is a reminder of the complexity of the task of understanding the changing patterns of faith and practice. In recognising the links which bind faith and culture, the book proposes to examine the changing profile of Irish religious belief patterns within the context of the emerging cultural patterns in the 'western' world. Readers will not be surprised to learn that there is no attempt to find that elusive vantage point that situates religious belief in a realm beyond culture. Instead, they will be invited to recognise the ways in which the Christian faith in Ireland has shaped and continues to influence the course of European culture and is, in turn, influenced by it.

A preview of papers

In the spring of 1996 the Mater Dei Institute hosted a series of public lectures and a weekend symposium on the theme 'Faith and Culture in the Irish Context'. The intention was to provide a forum for both scholars and members of the public to engage in a mutually enriching dialogue designed to situate the changes in Irish religious belief patterns in the context of the larger canvas symbolised by the phrase 'contemporary culture'.

In the opening essay in this collection, 'Faith and Culture: A Complex Relationship', Bishop Donal Murray presents us with a vision of culture which allows the reader to understand just why it is that the links between faith and culture are inevitable. Although not identical, religion and culture are two aspects of the human search for meaning. In the section entitled 'Who are we?', Murray draws the reader's attention to aspects of contemporary culture which can paradoxically suppress this quest for meaning. He sees in the phrase 'the culture of contempt' a way of describing this uniquely contemporary attempt to evade the question of human meaning and in that context recognises a task which unites culture and faith – the task of 'giving a soul to society'.

In the final section, entitled 'Culture and morality', Murray situates the links between faith and culture in the context of the question 'Is the universe ultimately compatible with liberty?' As he observes, 'Moral reflection begins with the same paradox as authentic culture – the paradox of the infinite in the finite, the spiritual in the material, the universal in the particular. If the paradox is evaded, then freedom either sees itself as swamped and helpless in the face of circumstances and events, or deludes itself into thinking that it is "unsituated" and unlimited.'

Murray concludes his essay by recognising that just as 'it is hard to imagine culture flourishing where there was no living faith and no moral urgency, it is equally unlikely that religion and morality could flourish for long in the absence of a healthy cultural life. But their unity, in the end, escapes our limited grasp'.

There follow three essays which address the challenges posed to religious faith by key aspects of contemporary culture: Fachtna McCarthy's 'The Mind of God: Science and Theology Today'; my own 'Religion and Culture: The Freedom to be an Individual'; and Michael Paul Gallagher's 'Post-modernity: Friend or Foe'.

Fachtna McCarthy alerts the reader to the salient truth that, as he puts it: 'One of the most fundamental challenges facing the Christian community at the beginning of the new millennium is the relationship between religion and science, the two strongest general forces which influence humanity'. Drawing on Herbert's classic work, *The Origins of Modern Science,* McCarthy observes that the scientific revolution of the seventeenth century was the most important landmark in western history since the rise of Christianity itself. Compared to the rise of science, the Renaissance and the Reformation were mere internal episodes, readjustments within the system of western Christianity. McCarthy continues: 'Even allowing for a certain rhetorical exaggeration, such comparisons raise obvious questions: What is the relationship between these two powerful cultural forces which have helped to shape the western mind? Are religion and science antagonistic or complementary? Has their relationship changed over time? What is the nature of their interaction today?'

McCarthy proposes three models to explain the historical development of the complex relationship between science and religion, that is, the conflict model, the separation model and the interaction model. In the course of his analysis of these models, he offers a unique insight into the contemporary dialogue between theology and science and allows the specialist in science access to a wide range of developments in contemporary scientific theory.

McCarthy concludes by proposing for our acceptance the interaction model. As he says: 'It is because they share a common origin in this fundamental human desire for the unity and coherence of all knowing that science and theology, while acknowledging their diversity, can never be allowed to go their separate ways. At the end of the century the new dialogue is revealing, not only potentially new, exciting and fruitful areas of mutual interest, but a greater humility and a sensitivity to the scope and limitations of each.'

In my own contribution, 'Religion and Culture: The Freedom to be an Individual', I focus upon that prominent feature of contemporary culture commonly referred to as Individualism. Many commentators have suggested that the apparent decline in religious sensibility in the 'western' world is in no small measure due to the rise of an individualist ethos, one which has its origins in the culture of the Enlightenment. While I do not wish to deny that Christianity, which places such emphasis on the love of God and the neighbour, is incompatible with an extreme individualist ethic, I am not, nevertheless, convinced that the contemporary desire to recover the experience of being an individual can be construed from a religious perspective in entirely negative terms. This essay was motivated both by the desire to understand this contemporary longing to be an individual and the need to reflect on the challenges which this movement poses for religious belief. In the course of the essay I reflect at some length on the multifaceted nature of individualism.

In the final essay in this grouping, 'Post-modernity: Friend or Foe?' Michael Paul Gallagher offers the reader a challenging excursus into the works of post-modernity and the opportunities which it offers for those concerned to propose a contemporary restatement of religious belief. I stress 'opportunities' because

Gallagher is concerned to highlight that, from a religious perspective, the legacy of post-modernity may not turn out to be as negative as many critics presume.

At the outset of his essay Gallagher acknowledges that the task of understanding post-modernity is not an easy one because as he says, 'it seems a chameleon word that changes its colours depending on the philosophy of the user'. It is commonly acknowledged, however, to be marked, both by a rejection of some of the more extreme forms of scientism or positivism associated with the modernist or enlightenment culture and a suspicion 'of the naive claims to progress, or insensitive dominance of the earth, or utopias about history'.

To facilitate the negotiation of this complex terrain, Gallagher provides the reader with a map or, more precisely, a diagram, which he entitles 'Faces of post-modernity'. What the diagram reveals is Gallagher's thesis that there are in fact two faces to post-modernity, one which he calls 'deconstructive' and the other 'constructive'. The deconstructive critique of modernity finds its ultimate expression in a nihilist world view, but the constructive critique has within it the possibility to facilitate a creative and liberating dialogue with those who are conscious of the religious horizons of meaning.

The essay concludes by outlining points of contact between religious belief and the constructive face of post-modernity such as ecology, feminism, and the return of spirituality and, also, by offering tentative pointers as to the direction in which this liberating dialogue might lead us.

The final four essays in this collection focus explicitly on an Irish context within which to study the relation between faith and culture. Michael Drumm's essay is entitled 'The Great Hunger – Shaping Irish Catholicism'. Two of the other essays are written with a view to discerning the changing patterns of religious beliefs and values in contemporary Irish society. The first is jointly written by Christopher T. Whelan and Tony Fahey of the

ESRI and is entitled 'Religious Change in Ireland, 1981-1990'. Uniquely, this essay is followed by a formal response from a philosophical perspective by Joseph Dunne, entitled 'Religion, and Modernity: Reading the Signs'. The final essay, by Marguerite Corish, is entitled, 'Aspects of the Secularisation of Irish Society 1958-1996'.

In his essay 'The Great Hunger – Shaping Irish Catholicism', Michael Drumm argues that in the dialogue between faith and culture insufficient attention has been paid to historical studies. In examining the importance of the Great Hunger of 1845-48 in shaping the religious consciousness of Irish Catholics, his paper makes no small contribution to the task of rectifying this imbalance. He reminds us that the contemporary expression of faith not only emerges in the context of the contemporary dialogue with culture but is chiselled out of the cultural legacy that is our history. Drumm argues that 'only when one gives due weight to the historical and theological consequences of this famine can one provide an adequate interpretation of many characteristics of the contemporary dialogue of faith and culture in the Irish context'.

His essay offers the reader access to the religious world of pre-Famine Ireland, where, as Drumm remarks, Irish Catholicism could be described as 'a traditional religion blending folk customs with Christian orthodoxy'. It was a world that was largely swept aside in the turmoil of post-Famine Ireland – a ferment exacerbated by the conflict between zealous Anglican evangelicals and the equally zealous Cardinal Cullen. Drumm argues cogently that the legacy of the Cullen reforms on the devotional character of Irish Catholicism up to and including the present can scarcely be over-stated.

As we take tentative steps to mark the one hundred and fiftieth anniversary of the Famine, it is salutary to be reminded that the centenary of the Famine in 1945-48 was scarcely acknowledged in Ireland. Drumm suggests that it is only at the present distance that we are able to recall the Famine experience and recognise the way it has shaped the cultural and religious heritage of the Irish people. In this context, the essay is both timely and valuable.

The essay 'Religious Change in Ireland, 1981-1990' is written jointly by Christopher T. Whelan and Tony Fahey. Their purpose is to present evidence from the European Values Surveys of 1981 and 1990 on religious values and behaviour in Ireland and to offer some comments on the overall significance of this evidence. They sift the evidence for indications of 'the pace and extent of change in religious adherence in Ireland' and they assert that the surveys can help 'to identify the sub-groups in the population where change has been most marked'. Consequently, the surveys offer insights into the impact of a range of social forces on religiosity in Ireland.

The European Values Surveys represent a thorough investigation into Irish social mores and are generally regarded as the authoritative barometers of social change in contemporary Ireland. Having been closely involved in the work of these Values Surveys, Whelan and Fahey are uniquely qualified to offer a trustworthy commentary on their findings.

The essay by Joseph Dunne is a response to Whelan and Fahey's paper. Its importance, however, transcends the limited, albeit valuable, parameters of a formal response. No serious study of cultural change ought to side-step the challenge of examining the methodological presumptions of the social sciences. Unfortunately, it is all too rare to find someone capable and willing to accept this indispensable task of critical analysis. Dunne's reflective essay not only challenges the unstated presuppositions of a survey such as that carried out under the auspices of the European Values Study but, in the process, highlights the merits of the careful analysis of the findings of this study by Whelan and Fahey. As he says, 'it is clear from Whelan and Fahey's paper [and in particular from the final section on 'Implications'] that they see the data collected in the Survey as being in need of interpretation and recognise that such interpretation, while it is of course constrained by the data [insofar as it is of them that it seeks to give a cogent account], must still go beyond them for its sources if it is to have anything adequate, let alone interesting or rich to offer'.

Dunne's essay broadens out into a philosophical analysis of selected features of the culture of modernity and reflects on their impact on the fortunes of religion in the modern world. In the course of this study which highlights the radically anthropocentric hue of modern culture, Dunne poses some particularly challenging questions to those occupied by the question of the future of the faith in the context of changes in contemporary culture.

The final essay in this publication, 'Aspects of the Secularisation of Irish Society 1958-1996' by Marguerite Corish, provides a valuable additional analytical assessment of recent social change in Ireland. Although complementing the work of Whelan and Fahey, it differs from their essay in a number of respects. Unlike them, Corish is concerned to examine a specific thesis, namely the appropriateness of using the term secularisation to describe the process of social change over the past forty years in Ireland. This difference in focus influences both the time-span examined and the choice of material analysed.

Considering that Corish is concerned to examine evidence of the secularisation of Irish society, there is a particular appropriateness in choosing the year 1958 to commence the study. Many commentators would agree with her that the socio-economic changes initiated by the publication in that year, of T. K. Whitaker's 'New Objectives of National Economic Policy', marked a sea change in Irish life – the beginnings of contemporary Ireland.

Drawing on a wide variety of survey material, Corish examines both the factors and agents of social change in Ireland over the past forty years. However, the essay is largely focused on an examination of the evidence for changes in patterns of religious practice in Ireland. Although many of the surveys examined are limited in comparison to the authoritative work produced in connection with the European Values Surveys of 1981 and 1900, nevertheless, as analysed by Corish, they offer the reader a valuable indication of the direction in which Irish society is heading as we approach the close of the second millennium.

NOTES

1. Joseph McGlade, *The Missions: Africa and The Orient,* Gill & Son, Dublin, 1967.
2. Ibid. p. 1.

FAITH AND CULTURE:
A COMPLEX RELATIONSHIP

Donal Murray

In his essay, *Notes towards the Definition of Culture,* T. S. Eliot is commendably frank about the complexity of the relationship between religion and culture: '... for the purposes of this essay, I am obliged to maintain two contradictory propositions: that religion and culture are aspects of one unity, and that they are different and contrasted things'.[1] I intend to reflect primarily on the first side of that 'contradiction'.

The encyclical *Centesimus annus* stresses the close bond between faith and culture in a passage which will form the foundation for this reflection:

> At the heart of every culture lies the attitude that the human being takes to the greatest mystery, the mystery of God. Different cultures are basically different ways of facing the question of the meaning of personal existence. When this question is eliminated, the culture and moral life of nations are corrupted.[2]

Every culture is based on a way or ways of facing the question of the meaning of human existence. That is a big claim, particularly in our day. Perhaps for the first time in history there is a widespread assumption that convictions about the meaning of existence are irrelevant not only to public life and public policy but even to basic cultural activities such as education.

Culture is not easily defined. I wish to use the word in the broadest sense, as it is used by Vatican II in *Gaudium et spes*. The human person develops only by means of culture, 'that is through the cultivation of the goods and values of nature'.[3] Wherever brute nature has been understood or shaped or celebrated, wherever people communicate, wherever human institutions and associations are established, wherever and however the universe is marked by the presence of human beings, there is culture.

That broad culture takes different forms:

> For different styles of living and different scales of values originate in different ways of using things, of working, of self-expression, of practising religion and of behaviour, of establishing laws and juridical institutions, of developing science and the arts and of cultivating beauty.[4]

The very heart of culture, therefore, is found in the ways by which human creativity and human freedom give shape and meaning to the world. The core of it lies in the relationship between the world which is given, which is there, which operates according to the unchanging laws of nature, and the human ability freely and creatively to cultivate that world. Free choice and creativity are both concerned with meaning.

It is, for instance, impossible to choose without a reason. Every free decision has a meaning. A free act is characterised by the fact that there is always some answer, however unreflected or implicit, to the question, 'Why did you do that?'[5]

Making discoveries
The first and most profound reason why faith and culture are two aspects of the same reality lies in the relationship between nature and freedom.

We find ourselves in a world not of our making. The universe operates in accordance with rules which we do not formulate and which we understand only imperfectly. There is a niggling question as to whether our only role is simply to resign ourselves to inevitable absurdity. Is the meaning which we imagine we can see in this reality nothing more than a comforting illusion?

That question reduces itself to this: Do we simply invent a meaning, or is culture the product of an effort, however imperfect and partial, to respond to a meaning which is there? Is human creativity simply doing a Rorschach Test, imposing sense on what is, in reality, only a jumble of blots, or does it, in the nuanced phrase we often use, 'make discoveries'?

Making implies doing something new; discovering implies bringing to light something which was already there. One is an active concept; the other is receptive. In the interplay of these two elements the human activity of giving meaning and shape to nature takes place. Both elements are essential. If the meaning we expressed echoed nothing in the real world, added nothing to our understanding of and interaction with the world as it is, then culture would be no more than an illusory escape from incoherence. If, on the other hand, the meaning is there to be uncovered, then the universe is not just an unyielding and purposeless machine.

And yet it is not simply a matter of uncovering a ready-made meaning which has been buried by a divine puzzle-setter – as if the universe were a kind of treasure hunt. The discovery must be *made;* it must be constructed. This has to happen in a world which I do not create out of nothing, but which I find already existing, a world in which I coexist with others who can, therefore, recognise the meaning I construct as *true.*

The most fundamental step in that construction of meaning is the individual human act of consent. A person may refuse to accept that human freedom is limited, that it has to be exercised in relationship with others, that it must operate in an existing world into which we are born. The situation in which freedom has to be exercised may be seen as a limitation; more fundamentally it is the sphere in which freedom may operate. A decision not to accept this reality, however freely that decision is taken and even if it is taken out of a passionate desire to be utterly untrammelled, is destructive of freedom.

Consent is the option by which I recognise the truth, and declare myself willing to accept the truth about myself and about the situation in which I exist and act. It is an option which cannot escape its religious implications.

> How can one justify the 'yes' of consent without passing a judgement on the value of the whole of the universe, that is, without appreciating its ultimate compatibility with liberty? Consent is not capitulation if, despite appearances, the world is the potential theatre of freedom. I say: 'This is my place, I adopt it; I do not surrender, I acquiesce; it is good thus; for 'all things work together for those who love God, for those who are called according to his purpose'. Thus consent would have its 'poetic' root in hope, as decision would have in love and as effort would have in the gift of the ability to act.[6]

The belief that the world is such that it provides the possibility of exercising liberty and creativity, implies some response of faith to the underlying question of meaning. But this is not simply to be identified with any particular religious creed. Religion and culture are two aspects of the human search for meaning, but they are not identical. They are also 'different and contrasted things'.

A religion, since it concerns the relationship of humanity, and of the entire universe, to God, ought to be capable of finding expression in every human culture. It should be wider and greater than any particular culture. If it is exclusively or overwhelmingly expressed in only one culture, then it is lacking something of the universality one might expect.

> A universal religion is at least potentially higher than one which any race or nation claims exclusively for itself; and a culture realising a religion also realised in other cultures

is at least potentially a higher culture than one which has a religion exclusively to itself. From one point of view we must identify: from another, we must separate.[7]

On the other hand, it is difficult to show any direct correspondence between the truth or nobility of a religion and the greatness of the culture in which it finds expression. The truth or falsity of a religion 'neither consists in the cultural achievements of the peoples professing that religion, nor submits to being exactly tested by them. For what a people may be said to believe, as shown by its behaviour, is... always a great deal more and a great deal less than its professed faith in its purity.'[8]

Art and culture have their origin not so much in answers to the question of meaning but in the intensity and honesty with which the question is faced. The best art is sometimes produced when religion appears to be in decline. Could this be the product of a passionate quest to recover a lost ability to address fundamentals? The deprivation of a sense of ultimate meaning may be felt most sharply in a society where a vision of faith has recently been widely shared; those who most acutely hear the question may be angry with traditional religion because they perceive it as failing in its role of providing satisfying and convincing answers.

Who are we?

The question of meaning has become crucial in our world; it is posed especially in terms of the meaning of personal existence: 'Who am I? Who are we? What does our life mean? Where does it lead?' Can we any longer see this world as the theatre of freedom, as a context in which our freedom is real and in which it makes sense? The highest cultural achievements are those which echo or which shed new light on that question, in literature or music or the visual arts.

Most of the time we live a kind of skeleton life. The question of the meaning of personal existence is firmly suppressed. We are surrounded by people who know us only in the role we play rather than as the full persons we are. When we meet people, it is usually on a purely functional level. Even those with whom we work closely – and this is especially true of men – may know nothing, and may want to know nothing, about our deepest questions, fears and hopes.

Successful business ventures, exciting sporting events, moments of joy and achievement can bring a passing sense of fulfilment; they cannot satisfy the longing to understand the meaning of life. Even the best personnel officer or human resource person will be of little help to an employee who, having reflected deeply on the meaning of life, asks 'What's the point of it all?'

There is a feeling of emptiness about modern life which expresses itself on the one hand in detachment, in an absence of real commitment to anything or anyone, and, on the other, in seeking after mysteries, cults and New Age ideas.

What is new in our time is that most of the activity that takes place in our culture appears not to be based on *any* answer to the question of the meaning of personal existence. Most of the contexts in which we find ourselves are such that it would sound extremely odd to ask 'What is life for?', and few would think that the answer would be likely to have any relevance to what they are doing.

So, for instance, the state increasingly sees itself as the provider of education, particularly the education of the young. But what is education? It is a process of preparing people for life. The State is capable of giving only the most limited answers to questions about the nature of the human person or the purpose of human life. Many different views exist on such questions among its citizens and the state has no way of choosing among those views. The fact that people can undertake the work of education without asking the questions and without thinking that the answers might have some relevance,

...is odd beyond all words. Yet it does not strike people as odd. And the depths of their unawareness of its oddness is the measure of the decay in thinking about fundamentals.[9]

So, for instance, anybody who claims that there are moral obligations which admit of no exception is regarded as 'absolutist' – although one notes that there are particular issues where even liberals are allowed to be absolutist. Generally speaking, however, anyone who regards a particular kind of behaviour as immoral is seen as being 'judgmental'. What is often not recognised is that such relativism is a necessary consequence of a failure to ask about the purpose of human life. If life has no overall purpose, there can be no overall vision of how to achieve the purpose.

It is no longer a question of atheism or even of agnosticism, both of which are ways of addressing the question of meaning. It is a question of trying to get along without asking the question at all.

One of the fruits which this produces is the contradiction in terms which has been described as 'the culture of contempt'. There is what the former Archbishop of York described as 'a contemptuous tone' in much of modern discourse,

> not only about the churches, but about other basic institutions in our society, the Monarchy, Parliament, even the Judiciary. Contempt hijacks understanding, it stops communication, it is less concerned with the truth than with demonstrating the author's cleverness.[10]

The 1990s have been a decade of disillusionment with structures and of the debunking of heroes. Some of this, no doubt, has been overdue and well-deserved, but it is not always evident that this debunking is a consequence of deep concern for truth and justice. Sometimes it is a consequence of believing that nothing matters, that nothing is admirable:

It cuts at the root of beliefs and attitudes and institutions which have traditionally held societies together. It discounts the accumulated wisdom of past generations. It sees history as no more than a record of human folly and corruption. Cynical contempt is one of the extreme forms of this rejection.[11]

Faith, on the contrary, is concerned with meaning and wholeness; it values the tradition in which it has been expressed and lived. The Gospel is fundamentally Good News, a deep amazement at human worth and dignity in the light of the incarnation and redemption.[12]

The religious impulse will always reveal itself as a search for wholeness, as a concern about one's roots, a longing for psychological and cultural individuality. Such preoccupations, never far away in modern writing, are the most obvious expression of the religious instinct in this turbulent Century.[13]

It is no coincidence that recent years have seen a great upsurge of interest in tracing one's roots. In a world which finds it hard to face questions like 'Who am I? Why do I matter? Will it make any difference in a hundred years that I lived at all?', it becomes more pressing to know where one fits in to something greater than oneself. It becomes important to see oneself as belonging, not as a cog in some great impersonal, uncaring machine, but as a living, organic part of the wider human family.

A world in which there is nothing worthy of belief or trust is a world which is lacking in inspiration. It is a world to which it is difficult to consent; it is a world which cannot easily be regarded as ultimately compatible with liberty. Unless human freedom has a goal which stretches it, unless it detects at least the possibility of a destiny which is worth the passionate and wholeheart-

ed commitment of personal resources, unless it faces the fundamental realities of life – birth, love, hope, vulnerability, fallibility
and death – there will be no culture worthy of the name. When
the question of the meaning of personal existence is eliminated
'the culture and moral life of nations are corrupted'.[14]

The cultural challenge which Europe faces is also a religious
challenge:

> The decline of ideologies, the erosion of confidence in the
> ability of structures to respond to the deeper problems and
> the anxious expectations of humanity, the dissatisfaction
> with an existence based on the ephemeral, the loneliness of
> the massive metropolises, the young abandoned to them-
> selves, and nihilism itself have created a huge vacuum
> which awaits credible heralds of new proposals of values
> capable of building any civilisation worthy of the human
> vocation... The Church is *called to give a soul to modern
> society.*[15]

This process has also been described as 'awakening us from our
"public unconsciousness" of spiritual reality'. Reawakening is
brought about particularly by writers like Dostoevsky, Camus
and Solzhenitsyn, who carry 'the authority of profound personal
truth' because 'they have opened themselves to the pull of transcendent reality'.[16]

Giving a soul to society

The giving of a soul to society is a task which unites culture and
faith. The truth of great art is not a merely particular, concrete
truth. It is universal. It reflects a deeper order, an ungraspable
mystery which underlies all truth. No event, no experience, no
insight can genuinely have meaning unless there is a greater
meaning within which it has a place. A bubble of meaning in a
universe of absurdity would itself be meaningless. The harmony

between this underlying mystery and the truth of the Gospel is clear:

> Christianity needs such words; it needs practice in learning to hear such words. For all its words would be misunderstood, if they were not heard as words of the mystery, as the coming of the blessed, gripping incomprehensibility of the holy.[17]

The unity of culture and faith is clear in that both are concerned with the full truth about the whole human person. Neither is exhausted by the merely rational, or the merely sentimental, or the merely functional, or the merely superficial. They deal with the depth of reality and with the heart of personal existence.

Neither religion nor culture could exist without some understanding of the unity of the human person. Culture is concerned with value and meaning expressed in material realities – in words and sounds and shapes and images. The wonder is that they can bear and communicate such profundities. Religion is concerned with transcendent, spiritual truths which must be expressed in limited and inadequate words and rituals.

The human condition is a magnificent tension in unity between the eternal and the temporal, the material and the spiritual. The human spirit is neither imprisoned in alien matter nor does it soar free; it is embodied; it is incarnate. The paradox which lies at the root both of culture and of faith is that the infinite is found in the finite, universality in the particular. The artist and the saint struggle to express the inexpressible, to know the unknowable – and in doing so, they both come to know themselves.

> It is in one single movement that a philosophy of the [human] subject and a philosophy of the transcendent are

worked out. The latter is, in the last resort, the philosophy of human limitations.[18]

) People's understanding of religion is often distorted by a strange fascination with 'the institutional Church'. The Church ought to be a place where human beings meet one another in the full truth of their humanity. It is precisely a context which is not primarily institutional. Where else in modern society do men and women gather, recognising their own mortality, admitting their own fallibility, acknowledging that universal justice and peace cannot be the fruit of human effort alone, realising that we cannot ultimately protect ourselves, or others, even the little children who depend on us and trust us, from illness and from the tragedies of life?

That, too, is the context in which art and high culture exist, in what has been called 'the long day's journey of the Saturday'. Between the tragedy and pain of Good Friday and the triumphant liberation of Easter lies the Saturday of waiting.

> The apprehensions and figurations in the play of metaphysical imagining, in the poem and the music, which tell of pain and hope, of the flesh which is said to taste of ash and of the spirit which is said to have the savour of fire, are always Sabbatarian. They have risen out of the immensity of waiting which is that of man. Without them, how could we be patient?[19]

In the Church we are united in the light of the response of faith to the deepest human questions. That is why it is such a sad impoverishment to think of the Church as a mere structure, an institution. It is a way, *the* way, of being fully human, of facing the question of who we are, not with a cynical or superficial dismissal but with transforming hope.

There is harmony between religion and culture because both

point to a meaning which is not fully grasped and not fully achieved. Scientists have become fascinated with the thought of a unified theory which would embrace all the laws of physics and of the whole of science. But even that, as Stephen Hawking pointed out, would not be the end of the human quest for meaning.

> If we discover a complete theory, it should in time be understandable in broad principle by everyone, not just a few scientists. Then we shall all, philosophers and scientists, and just ordinary people, be able to take part in the discussion of why it is that we and the universe exist. If we find the answer to that, it would be the ultimate triumph of human reason – for then we would know the mind of God.[20]

That is the key question. It asks what our life and our world mean. Why has the world come into existence and where does life lead? 'The two questions, the first about the origin and the second about the end, are inseparable. They are decisive for the meaning and orientation of our lives and actions.'[21]

Culture and morality

The issue of meaning is fundamental for the understanding of morality. The encyclical *Veritatis splendor* begins from the question of the rich young man (Mt 19:16-21).

> For the young man, the question is not so much about the rules to be followed, but *about the full meaning of life*. This is in fact the aspiration at the heart of every human decision and action, the quiet searching and interior prompting which sets freedom in motion. This question is ultimately an appeal to the absolute Good which attracts us and beckons us; it is the echo of a call from God who is the origin and goal of human life.[22]

The most fundamental cultural question is also the most fundamental moral question: 'Is the universe ultimately compatible
with liberty?' The supreme purpose of life is what sets freedom in
motion and explains why we make any choice at all.[23]

In the light of Christian revelation, one can go further. We
speak of human creativity in relation to the great works of culture. But only God can create in the strict sense. Human creativity 'makes discoveries'; it does not bring something into existence
out of nothingness. At the same time, human creativity is founded on God's act of creation:

> ... our creativity is indeed an echo of that unique divine
> creation. God created from freedom, in goodness, and in
> love, and our cultural creativity is born from that gift.[24]

The 'contradiction' of union and difference between culture and
faith reaches a particular sharpness in the relationship between
culture and morality. If one attempts to relate them in too sim-
plistic a fashion, making facile moral judgements about works of
art, one may end up burning books. If one attempts to separate
them completely, then morality risks becoming cold and empty,
unable to echo the hope and tragedy of human life, while culture
is in danger of becoming amoral, dehumanised and open to
being enlisted in the service of evil causes.

Granted the complexity of the relationship, it is interesting to
reflect that the requirements of a sound moral theology as set out
in *Veritatis Splendor* are also requirements for authentic culture.
Morality, like culture, is founded on a proper understanding of
the relationship between nature and freedom.

> *Debates about nature and freedom* have always marked the
> history of moral reflection; they grew especially heated at
> the time of the Renaissance and the Reformation, as can
> be seen from the teaching of the Council of Trent. Our

own age is marked, though in a different sense, by a similar tension. The penchant for empirical observation, the procedures of scientific objectification, technological progress and certain forms of liberalism have led to these two terms being set in opposition, as if a dialectic, if not an absolute conflict, between freedom and nature were characteristic of the structure of human history.[25]

It is in the unity of body and soul that the person is free. Human freedom does not create its own universe. It acts in the situation of time and space in which it finds itself, by choosing among possibilities which it recognises, with abilities which the person possesses or acquires, for reasons which suggest themselves. Human freedom is not a capacity to escape from reality but a capacity to deal truthfully with reality. We are inserted in reality because we are embodied; we can deal with reality because we are embodied. The human body is not simply one material thing among the objects that exist, it is also a subject, an 'I'. My hand or my foot is part of what I mean by 'me'.

Moral reflection begins with the same paradox as authentic culture – the paradox of the infinite in the finite, the spiritual in the material, the universal in the particular. If the paradox is evaded then freedom either sees itself as swamped and helpless in the face of circumstances and events or deludes itself into thinking that it is 'unsituated' and unlimited. The reality is that our freedom has a meaning which we do not create out of nothing, as if the human body was 'a raw datum, devoid of any meaning or moral values until freedom has shaped it':

> The person, by the light of reason and the support of virtue, discovers in the body the anticipatory signs, the expression and the promise of the gift of self, in conformity with the wise plan of the Creator.[26]

29

One does not blame an earthquake or an avalanche for the damage it causes. Human actions are not mere events in the physical world. They give rise to moral questions because they express human intentions and meanings.

> In order to be able to grasp the object of an act which specifies that act morally, it is therefore necessary to place oneself in the perspective of the acting person.... By the object of a given moral act, then, one cannot mean a process or an event of the purely physical order, to be assessed on the basis of its ability to bring about a given state of affairs in the outside world.[27]

Morality, like culture, is a way of 'facing the question of the meaning of personal existence'.[28] A free choice is always to a greater or lesser degree an answer to the question, 'Who am I?'

> It has been rightly pointed out that freedom is not only the choice for one or another particular action; it is also, within that choice, a decision about oneself and a setting of one's own life for or against the Good, for or against the Truth, and ultimately for or against God.[29]

The encyclical stresses that this fundamental decision or option about oneself and about the meaning of one's life is not to be separated from the more mundane aspects of freedom.

> To separate the fundamental option from concrete kinds of behaviour means to contradict the substantial integrity or personal unity of the moral agent....[30]

The moral action is also a decision about others. My treatment of another person makes a statement about how I regard that person. We saw that one of the characteristic aspects of our culture is that human relationships become increasingly functional and anonymous. The morality of the Gospel demands a readiness to rise, like the Good Samaritan, above the expected and the obligatory. It is no longer a matter of imposed duties but of love.

> Love of neighbour springs from a loving heart which, precisely because it loves, is ready to live out the loftiest challenges.[31]

Conclusion

The 'contradiction' of unity and difference between morality and culture raises many questions. It is evident that they need each other. It is hard to imagine culture flourishing where there was no living faith and no moral urgency; it is equally unlikely that religion and morality could flourish for long in the absence of a healthy cultural life. But their unity, in the end, escapes our limited grasp.

> To judge a work of art by artistic or by religious standards, to judge a religion by religious or artistic standards should come in the end to the same thing: though it is an end at which no individual can arrive.[32]

It is, nevertheless, fascinating that when the Pope wished to outline the frame of mind which is required in order to celebrate the Gospel of life which is 'at the heart of Jesus' message' and which tells of 'the greatness and inestimable value of human life even in its temporal phase',[33] he described 'a contemplative outlook' which might also serve as a description of the conditions for cultural creativity:

> It is the outlook of those who see life in its deeper meaning, who grasp its utter gratuitousness, its beauty and its invitation to freedom and responsibility. It is the outlook

31

of those who do not presume to take possession of reality but instead accept it as a gift, discovering in all things the reflection of the Creator and seeing in every person his living image. This outlook does not give in to discouragement when confronted by those who are sick, suffering, outcast or at death's door. Instead, in all these situations it feels challenged to find meaning, and precisely in these circumstances it is open to perceiving in the face of every person a call to encounter, dialogue and solidarity.[34]

Perhaps in that contemplative outlook we may yet create a new European evangelisation and a revitalised European culture. The dream of European unity or integration cannot work unless Europe once again finds a soul, unless, if I may misquote Seamus Heaney, 'faith and culture rhyme'.

The Second Vatican Council called Christians to a unity of life, overcoming the separation of 'faith from life, and the Gospel from culture'. In endorsing that call, Pope John Paul maintains 'that a faith that does not affect a person's culture is a faith "not fully embraced, not entirely thought out, not faithfully lived" '.[35]

NOTES

1. T. S. Eliot, *Notes towards the Definition of Culture*, London, Faber & Faber, 1962 (2nd edition), p. 68.
2. John Paul II, *Centesimus annus* (1991), 24.
3. Vatican II, *Gaudium et spes*, 53.
4. *Gaudium et spes*, loc.cit.
5. '...il n'y a pas d'acte sans responsabilité; et il suit immédiatement de là que les mots *acte gratuite* sont en réalité contradictoires'. [There is no act without responsibility; and it follows immediately from that that the words *gratuitous act* are in fact contradictory]. Cf. G. Marcel, *Essai de Philosophie Concrète*, Paris, Gallimard, 1967, p. 164.
6. P. Ricoeur, *Le Volontaire et l'Involontaire*, Paris, Aubier, 1967,

p. 439: 'Comment justifier le oui du consentement sans porter un jugement de valeur sur l'ensemble de l'univers, c'est-à-dire sans en apprécier l'ultime convenance à la liberté? Consentir n'est point capituler si malgré les apparences le monde est le théâtre possible de la liberté. Je dis: voici mon lieu, je l'adopte; je ne cède pas, j'acquiesce; cela est bien ainsi; car 'toutes choses concourent au bien de ceux qui aiment Dieu, de ceux qui sont appelés selon son dessein'.

Ainsi le consentement aurait sa racine 'poétique' dans l'espérance, comme la décision dans l'amour et l'effort dans le don de force.'

7. T. S. Eliot, op. cit., p. 31.
8. T. S. Eliot, op. cit., p. 33.
9. F. Sheed, *Society and Sanity,* London, Sheed & Ward, 1953, pp. 3, 4.
10. J. Habgood, The Priestland Memorial Lecture, BBC Radio 4, Sunday, 8 October 1995.
11. Ibid.
12. John Paul II, *Redemptor Hominis,* 1979, 10.
13. D. Egan, *The Death of Metaphor,* Newbridge, The Kavanagh Press, 1990, p. 133.
14. John Paul II, *Centesimus annus,* 24.
15. John Paul II, Address to Sixth Symposium of the Council of European Episcopal Conferences, *Osservatore Romano,* English edition, 21 October 1985.
16. D. Walsh, *After Ideology: Recovering the Spiritual Foundations of Freedom,* San Francisco, Harper & Row, 1990, p. 4.
17. K. Rahner, 'Poetry and the Christian', *Theological Studies IV,* London, Darton, Longman & Todd, 1966, p. 359.
18. P. Ricoeur, op. cit., p. 440: 'C'est d'un seul mouvement que se détermine une philosophie du sujet et une philosophie de la Transcendance, laquelle en dernier ressort est la philosophie des confins de l'homme.'
19. G. Steiner, *Real Presences,* London, Faber & Faber, 1989, p.232.

20. S. Hawking, *A Brief History of Time*, London, Bantam Press, p. 175.
21. *Catechism of the Catholic Church*, Dublin, Veritas Publications, 1994, par. 282.
22. John Paul II, *Veritatis splendor*, 1993, 7.
23. See Aquinas, *Summa Theologiae I-II*, q.1, a.6c.
24. P. Poupard, 'Creation, Culture and Faith', *The Furrow*, May 1995, p. 276.
25. John Paul II, *Veritatis splendor*, 46.
26. John Paul II, *Veritatis splendor*, 48.
27. John Paul II, *Veritatis splendor*, 78.
28. John Paul II, *Centesimus annus*, 24.
29. John Paul II, *Veritatis splendor*, 65.
30. John Paul II, *Veritatis splendor*, 67.
31. John Paul II, *Veritatis splendor*, 15.
32. T. S. Eliot, op. cit., p. 30.
33. John Paul II, *Evangelium vitae*, 1995, 1, 2.
34. John Paul II, *Evangelium vitae*, 83.
35. John Paul II, *Christifideles laici*, 1988, 59.

THE MIND OF GOD:
SCIENCE AND THEOLOGY TODAY

Fachtna McCarthy

One of the most fundamental challenges facing the Christian community at the beginning of the new millennium is the relationship between religion and science, the 'two strongest general forces which influence humanity'.[1] In the preface to his classic work, *The Origins of Modern Science,* Herbert Butterfield drew a startling parallel. The scientific revolution of the seventeenth century was the most important landmark in western history since the rise of Christianity itself. Compared to the rise of science, the Renaissance and the Reformation were mere internal episodes, readjustments within the system of western Christianity.[2] Even allowing for a certain rhetorical exaggeration, such comparisons raise obvious questions: what is the relationship between these two powerful cultural forces which have helped to shape the western mind? Are religion and science antagonistic or complementary? Has their relationship changed over time? What is the nature of their interaction today?

As we come to the end of the millennium there can be no denying which force is in the ascendancy. Scientific rationality to a great extent provides the theoretical base for what our culture accepts as knowledge. In Walter Kasper's phrase, the natural sciences provide us with the 'hard core of modernity.'[3] Popular culture has given science an almost sacred character, its practitioners held in awe as mediating the mysteries of the natural world to us. Science has transformed our map of the physical universe and dominates our daily lives by its amazingly successful applications. How can we not have faith in science when it has produced the technology that underpins everything from our economy, our

35

health and our life-styles? The attempt to portray the relationship between science and religion today appears one-sided: for many in the scientific world religious faith is an anachronism, a pre-scientific answer to questions now best answered by science; the scientific enterprise provides the dynamic engine of change, constantly revising its conclusions and pushing back the boundaries of knowledge. By comparison, religious faith seems outdated, vague and mythological; for many science has replaced religion as the primary source of authority and meaning. Hence Christian theology, the systematic reflection on faith, appears to be in continuous retreat before a cumulative and infallible scientific method. Is it possible to take religion seriously in an age of science?

What is surprising, then, is the re-emergence of God within the intellectual horizon of late twentieth-century science. One contemporary effort is the re-asking of the God-question as an intelligible question, not within a traditional theological matrix, but within the orbit of scientific discussion about the natural world. My title is taken from the final sentence of Stephen Hawking's best-seller, *A Brief History of Time,* in which he claims that the ultimate goal of theoretical physics is to 'know the mind of God'.[4] Our positive reaction to such a development, that science has become open to the question of God, for so long blocked by the positivist and reductionist prejudices of this century, should be tempered with a certain caution. For Hawking 'God' is not the gracious and personal God of Christian theology, but, rather ambivalently, the 'embodiment of the laws of physics'.[5] The physicist Paul Davies claims that science has advanced to the point where what formerly were theological questions can now be properly tackled. He asserts that 'science offers a surer path to God than religion' in the sense that it could arrive more securely at a sense of the divine reality without relying on the claims of an ambiguous religious tradition.[6] *The New York Times Magazine* declares that 'God's turf' now belongs not to the theologian, but to the scientist.'[7] Should we beware of scientists bearing gifts? Is science predatory, attempting a takeover of theology's traditional territory, but doing it more subtly now than in the past? Is science attempting to steal the theologians' clothes?

The last twenty years has seen an exceptional upsurge in the interaction between science and theology. What is quite remarkable is that the dialogue has stemmed mostly from scientists in their writings of popular quasi-theological works. For the most part, the dialogue partners belong to the disciplines of theoretical physics and cosmology, that is, with contemporary theories concerned with the origin and structure of the universe as a whole. Many of these scientists, like Hawking, have no explicit commitment to religious faith; they challenge traditional theological concepts, in particular the nature of God and his action in the world, and replace them with their own quasi-religious views generated within the context of their science.

Another group of scientists, who are Christians, invest their energies in teasing out the theological implications of their disciplines. They belong to a new breed, the scientist-theologian whose expertise straddles the divide, being at home in both realms.[8] The very extensive interdisciplinary literature of the last twenty years attests to the vibrant and energetic dialogue between both groups and among themselves. What are the kinds of question at issue in their debates? They cover a very broad spectrum arising from physics, cosmology, biology and genetics. How can we understand our universe as God's creation? If the natural world is the province of the scientists how can theologians continue to speak intelligibly of creation without taking modern natural science into account? What possible implications do new scientific discoveries and theories have for our understanding of God's relationship to the world? Does science rule out a personal God? Did the universe somehow create itself, so obviating the need for a Creator-God? Does the world display purpose or design or is it the product of blind chance? In an autonomous universe, adequately explained in terms of the laws of physics, what room is there for the action of God? These questions constitute the central problematic for the interaction of science and theology today; they evoke a wide range of responses by the various participants in the dialogue. In order to narrow the focus of this paper, I propose to survey the various ways that theology and science are related to one another today. Such a typology, it is hoped, will provide an overview of a very complex interdisciplinary field; it betrays the weakness of any attempt at generalisation, the broad brush may sweep everything into neat bundles where precision and clarity may suffer. There are three principal ways or models of understanding the relationship between theology and science today: these models are conflict, separation and interaction.[9] The models could be understood historically in the sense of a progression in our understanding of their relationship over time; yet all three, in various forms, are still operative today.

Models of the relationship between science and religion
1. *The conflict model*
The conflict model suggests a deep and abiding antipathy between both which can only be overcome by the suppression of one by the other, that theology is an implacable enemy of science or that science invalidates religion. This 'warfare' view is based on a certain interpretation of the often stormy history of science and religion. Ever since the infamous trial of Galileo, it is claimed that religion and science are on an inevitable collision course, that the religious interpretation of the world cannot be reconciled with the discoveries of science. That battle reached its height with Darwin's evolutionary theory in the nineteenth century which resulted in an extreme polarisation of the Church and the scientific community in the falling-out over evolutionary theory. Theology and science are locked in a fight to the death over the same intellectual territory. The same fundamental questions are at stake; there can be only one winner.

Scientism is clear concerning the victor in the conflict: science provides us with the only reliable knowledge about our world and the only reliable method in the search for truth. What science cannot tell us we cannot know. What science tells us is that matter is the only fundamental reality in the universe and everything is reducible to matter or energy. This reductionist view holds that any whole system can be exhaustively explained by a cumulative account of its component parts. So a human being is essentially a complex deterministic mechanism fully understood by the laws of physics and chemistry; he or she is nothing but a physico-chemical system. On this view, science provides an exhaustive description of reality, it is an alternative 'faith', scientific materialism. Theology fails the test of scientific verification and is dismissed as pseudo-knowledge which must be excluded from the temple of learning. Science constantly tests all its hypotheses and theories against experience but theology cannot provide concrete, irrefutable evidence for the existence of God. Theology is subjective, emotional, invested with personal commitment, whereas science is neutral, objective and disinterested. Carl Sagan, the popular writer on astronomy, illustrates this position when he claims: 'The Cosmos is all that is or ever will be'.[10] God is replaced by nature as the object of awe and reverence. For many young people the conflict model has resolved the issues for them: science is about hard public facts, religion fails this test and is a matter of private personal preference.

A basic defect of scientism is that God and nature are placed on the same level as competitors, working on the assumption that anything attributed to God has to be denied to nature and vice versa.[11] That is to deny the theological understanding of God's transcendence, to ignore the ontological gap between creature and Creator. Furthermore, scientism has uncritically passed over the boundary between physics and metaphysics. To claim that a human being is 'nothing but' a piece of biological machinery is a metaphysical claim, invalidly added on to a legitimate scientific description in biology. Many working scientists are unreflective and implicit reductionists, according to Arthur Peacocke.[12] The methodological necessities of scientific analysis are agnostic in that God is not an element in scientific explanation. This heuristic necessity may pass over into a hard metaphysical world-view; because God is methodologically excluded from the parts, he does not exist in the whole. On ultimate questions concerning the meaning of the whole, science is systematically silent; these are not scientific questions. A similar criticism of scientism is proposed by Ian Barbour:[13] a particular scientific theory has become 'inflated' into an all-embracing naturalistic philosophy. There can be no warrant to claiming that a scientific theory provides an exhaustive description of reality; other levels of description and explanation cannot be ruled out a priori. Higher functions cannot be completely understood in terms of lower functions, the whole is greater than the parts. Those elements which get left out in scientific description, for example love, friendship, emotion, aesthetic sensibility, tend to be defined as less real than the mathematical equations which describe the world in which they arise. Scientism absolutises a form of knowledge that is legitimate in its own sphere. To mistake a part for the whole is every bit as fundamentalist as religious fundamentalism, the subject of our next section.

The other and opposite outcome of the conflict model sees religion as the victor. If there is a conflict between faith and science then science must be wrong. Creation scientists or creationists, mostly to be found in the Southern States of the United States, take their stand on the literal truth of the Bible. Creationists are the heirs to an older fundamentalism but there is a marked difference between them. Fundamentalists claim that the revered Word of God, which is inerrant throughout, is the highest truth and takes precedence over human discoveries; hence science which conflicts with the Bible is rejected on theological grounds. Creationists, on the other hand, interpret the Bible as a book of science. Biblical truth and scientific truth are of the same kind and are in direct competition as to the best scientific explanation. So evolutionary theory is rejected because the account of creation in the book of Genesis is a more adequate scientific theory about how the world and humans were created. God fixed distinct species at the moment of creation; they did not evolve over biological time by a process of natural selection, as evolution claims. Creationists claim that there is extensive geological and biological evidence to support their view.[14] This conflation of science into religion is a threat both to the autonomy of science and to religious freedom. Creationists fail to recognise the gulf that separates the mind-set of the ancient world in the Bible from that of modern scientific mentality.[15] Their literal interpretation of the Bible misconstrues the meaning and purpose of revelation and lacks any support from the broad consensus of contemporary biblical criticism.

An extremely negative view of science is often allied to the religious supremacy position. Science has not only produced a godless universe, but it has succeeded in destroying human meaning and value as well.[16] All modern ills can be laid at the door of science and its technological applications: the alienation and dehumanisation found in industrial societies, the nuclear threat, ecological disasters and the pollution and exploitation of nature. Science has wrested all mystery from the cosmos and reduced humans to machines, in order to control and manipulate the world. This destructive, apocalyptic vision of science is nicely illustrated by the words Goethe put in the mouth of Faust: 'That what we need to know we never will, And what we *do* know, we can only use to kill.'[17] In this extremely pessimistic view, both the spirit and the logic of science are anti-religious, corrosive of transcending human values and culture. Neither fundamentalism, scientism or creationism, occupies the central ground today, as they each once did in the era of post-Darwinian controversy.

2. *The separation model*

In recent decades many have argued that the conflict model reveals a fundamental misunderstanding of the real nature of science and theology and a false reading of their history.[18] Only the strict compartmentalisation of both disciplines does justice to both. Science and theology have carved out separate intellectual territories with clearly defined boundaries. We should not judge religion by the standards of science, nor science by the standards of religion. They each have very dissimilar tasks, they ask different questions, their methods are different and they recognise their limitations. Conflict occurs only when science or theology fails to respect the proper terrain of the other. There is no intrinsic contradiction between Christian faith and natural science; science can neither prove nor disprove the existence of God, as God is not a material object. One way of putting the separation case is to assert that science and religion speak two different languages which are complementary, but there can be no real conflict as they occupy totally disparate domains of knowledge. Science deals with objective or public knowing of proximate causes whereas theology deals with existential or personal knowing of ultimate causes. Theology raises fundamental questions about the ultimate ground of reality and affirms God as that absolute ground. Science asks *how* things happen in nature, but religion asks *why* there is something rather than nothing; science deals with soluble problems whereas religion is concerned with impenetrable mystery. The language of science concerns itself with the prediction and control of the material universe; religion is a commitment to a way of life, to a set of moral norms based on God's revelation in history, above all in the person of Jesus Christ.[19] Since there is no abiding conflict between Christian faith and scientific method the goal today is to be bilingual.[20]

The separation model has distinct advantages over the conflict model, not least in that the atmosphere is calmer, putting to

42

rest the heated confrontations of the past. The argument goes that, only by envisaging science and religion as independent, autonomous ways of knowing can we prevent the antagonism and the warfare between them. A clear line of demarcation appears to be the logical way out of past misunderstandings, a solution to the impasse reached by scientism on the one hand and creationism on the other. Hence, scientism, the philosophical faith that science provides the only objective knowledge about our world, and not science as such, is the true enemy of religious faith. The lessons of biblical criticism suggest that the Bible is not a book of science but a sacred text with a religiously inspired message couched in the language of symbol and myth.

Whilst recognising the benefits of the separation model, it is no longer uncritically accepted by many scientists and theologians today. The paradigm of separate intellectual territories ignores, not only the unity of all knowledge, but the actual historical relations between theology and science. The influence goes both ways; theology has always been swayed by prevailing scientific theories and philosophical world-views.[21] Historians record that theological presuppositions, often not explicitly articulated, were frequently woven into scientific theories. It has often been claimed that the Christian doctrine of creation provided the theological underpinning for the rise of the experimental sciences in the sixteenth century.[22] By grounding the natural order in the rationality of a personal God, Christian theology laid the foundations for the scientist's 'faith' in the order and coherence of the material universe. The argument runs that because God freely creates, the world is contingent, it is not necessary; it could have been otherwise and therefore its character cannot be deduced from first principles, as the Greek philosophers thought. Hence empirical inquiry and hands-on testing provide the only reliable ways of discovering how the world works. Furthermore, the world is orderly and shows rational symmetry and predictability since it was created by a good, intelligent Creator. The corollary is that human beings, created in the image and likeness of God, can understand the universe created by God, that the workings of nature are accessible to the human mind. Because there exists an ontological distinction between the creature and the Creator, the world is not God and so we are morally free to experiment with the world. The 'de-divinisation' of the universe means it can now be understood as an autonomous entity. Divorced from their theological base in the existence of God, these assumptions, contingency, rationality and accessibility, continue to underlie the practice of science today.[23] The interaction between science and religion has always been going on but may not be explicitly recognised.

3. *The interaction model*

Today there is among theologians and scientists alike an on-going attempt to rethink the relationship between science and theology. The separation model does not do full justice to the complexity of a whole range of issues in the interface between both. Separate domains, separate ghettos of learning insulated by high walls are no longer tenable. The unity and coherence of all knowing and the growing consciousness of living in one inter-connected world means that, though science and theology are logically and linguistically distinct disciplines, they can no longer be artificially insulated from one another as they are both trying to understand the same reality. Now that the heat and passion have gone out of the old debates, there is a new interest in dialogue, in the search for points of contact, for parallels in their methods, for areas of overlap. The situation today is described by David Tracy as 'a search for significant similarities and differences between the scientific and religious dimensions of our common humanity'.[24] The interaction model proposes a mutually beneficial dialogue: scientific knowledge can broaden the horizon of religious faith and the perspective of religious faith can deepen our understanding of the universe.

Science can benefit theology by bringing to light implicit cosmological assumptions in theology, such as a geocentric universe, which are no longer tenable. Different cosmologies provide different contexts for theological thought, and a theology which fits one historical cosmology may not be adequate for contemporary changes in our picture of the world. The kind of world described by big bang physics and evolutionary biology, for example, is not compatible with the God of Newton or Descartes. The religious quest of human beings cannot but be affected by this new twentieth-century scientific perspective on where we have come from and the processes that have led to our being here at all.

Theology can benefit science by bringing to light the philosophical presuppositions of science; these are not amenable to the scientific enterprise. Science makes an 'act of faith' in its presuppositions: that the material entities it observes are real, existing independently of the observer, that these entities have a coherent rationality, and that they are governed by consistent laws discoverable by us. The meta-questions, which science raises but does not answer, can receive a satisfactory response within a religious framework. Two limit or boundary situations in science which raise religious questions are described by Walter Kasper: the conditions for the possibility of scientific inquiry and the moral responsibility of scientists when faced with the implications of their research, especially in the area of genetics and the threat of nuclear power.[25]

The scientist-theologians are agreed on the need for science and theology to interact with one another, to find a mutual consistency in their accounts of reality, but they disagree on what that requires in practice. But Barbour, Peacocke and others want to go beyond a search for coherence and consistency between theology and scientific theory. They ask whether, in principle, it is possible to reformulate some particular Christian doctrines, like the doctrine of creation, in the light of the findings of cosmology and evolution.[26] What is at issue is the degree to which theology should accommodate itself to contemporary scientific findings. A delicate situation arises: to attempt to reformulate theology's central convictions in the light of a fluid and changing scientific picture of the world may make it a hostage to fortune, to the provisional findings of science. Theology cannot rely too heavily on science, yet it has to be open to what is going on in contemporary physics, chemistry and biology. In refusing to relate to contemporary science, theology risks abdicating its contribution to public discourse, to making claims about the nature of the real, and retreats instead into the ghetto of a private faith. Immunising theology against what is going on in science is fatal to its intellectual integrity, as theology may appear to be what its detractors in the conflict model claim, an irrational mythological stance on the world.[27]

This new creative interaction between science and theology has sometimes been called 'consonance'.[28] Consonance means the search for a harmony or a correspondence between what can be said by the latest science about the cosmos and what the theologian understands to be God's creation. Consonance is inspired by, among other things, recent philosophical discussions comparing the nature and methods of science with those of theology. The ways of science and theology do not appear to be nearly so divergent as the separation or conflict model would have it. Science is no longer considered to be as objective and detached as the separation model suggests; neither is theology seen as subjective and non-evidential. Science and theology share certain characteristics: both science and theology are concerned with the search for truth, and they employ models, theories and metaphors to interpret their data. Arthur Peacocke draws strong parallels between scientific and theological method. Theology has data constituted by the religious experience of a community and so should attempt to give the best explanation according to the 'normal criteria of reasonableness: fit with the data, internal coherence, comprehensiveness and general cogency'.[29]

The new interest of science in theological questions has been given impetus, not so much by the Churches, but by new discoveries in the sciences. The scientific community is currently engaged in a search for new paradigms. The debate pivots on whether classical Newtonian physics is adequate for explaining the behaviour of all material phenomena in the world. The mechanical clockwork model of the universe – entirely predictable and ruled by rigid invariant laws – has broken down because of the uncertainties at the level of quantum physics and because of the unpredictability of chaotic systems.[30] At the level of elementary particles of matter there is randomness, unpredictability and choice; here scientific research can only work with statistical probabilities and not with hard laws of predictability. The deterministic picture of the world, which positivism inherited from Newton's universal laws, is also called into question because of the unexpected and creative events that emerge from understanding nature as more like a living organism. Many present day scientists see themselves with their bodies, minds and emotions as part of a living cosmos, which one must approach with respect and empathy, even as a scientist. We and the universe belong to one family, united beyond the Cartesian dualism of mind and body.[31] The effect of Descartes' dualism, underpinning Newton's universe, split the world into inert material stuff, the object of science, and pure subjectivity, the free thinking spirit.[32] A closed autonomous universe was no longer the theatre of God's activity; nature was no longer the book that revealed God, and although Newton tried to save the world for God, a gradual unstoppable erosion of God from the universe followed. Religious thinkers were reduced to seeking God in the gaps of scientific theories and as these gaps were increasingly filled God became redundant. Nature contained no unfathomable mysteries that were not transparent to rational analysis, expressible in mathematical language. Historically this led to the God of deism, a God reduced to creating and winding up the clock of universe, but once under way he played no further part in it.[33] God is reduced to absolute transcendence and his immanence in the world is effectively undermined. Such a narrow scientific rationality based on the Newtonian universe has been increasingly questioned today, not least by scientists themselves.

A fruitful area, then, of the debate between science and theology concerns the kind of knowing they each represent – this turns out to be as much a challenge to science as it is to theology. The popular view of science in scientific textbooks, that science is purely objective, neutral and disinterested in its method of analysing the world, now appears naive. Philosophers of science have pointed out the social nature of all knowledge and the historical, cultural and social nature of scientific understanding. Thomas Kuhn, in his study *The Structures of Scientific Revolutions*, holds that theories and data in science are both strongly dependent on the dominant paradigm of the scientific community.[34] Paradigm is defined as a cluster of metaphysical, conceptual and methodological presuppositions embodied in a certain tradition of scientific work, such as the paradigm of the Newtonian mechanical universe. Science as the view from nowhere and the scientist as the detached observer of pristine facts are no longer viable. Scientific research is not value-free, it is not a detached pursuit of pure knowledge; science and scientists exist in a socio-political context which influences their work.[35] Kuhn points out that scientific textbooks tend to mask the conflicts and disagreements that underlie the growth of scientific understanding. The philosophical consensus today is that there are no uninterpreted facts: in the words of Ian Barbour, 'the data of science are theory laden, not theory free'.[36] Our theories influence our selection and interpretation of what we take to be data; what counts as fact depends on the prior expectation of our theory. Theories are creative leaps of the imagination in which models and analogies have a role to play. The observer is a participant, an active agent in an interactive system. Scientific theories provide us with a point of view, so it is important to ask from which point of view we are operating. A critical realism holds that our scientific and theological understandings both give us knowledge about the real world, whether the universe or God, but precisely because neither the universe nor God can ever be exhausted by the human mind, our thoughts in theology and science are always open to correction. Science cannot demonstrate that a physical explanation is the complete or the only explanation.[37] There are various levels of description of reality and the scientific is not the only one possible.

A further important consequence of the contemporary interaction between theology and science is that it has encouraged theology to broaden the scope and range of its concerns. Modern theology has conceded the natural world to the sciences; though our Christian creed proclaims that God is the 'Creator of heaven and earth', our theology has neglected this cosmic truth. Some theology has been narrow and parochial, preoccupied solely with questions of human beings in the context of salvation history.[38] Moltmann points out that the prestige given to science as pure knowledge and as the engine of progress has adversely affected theology. Theology has withdrawn to the field of history, leaving nature exclusively to the scientists.[39] In a renewed theology of creation it is imperative to recover the immanence of God in creation. For Moltmann, the new cosmology is a spur to recover something of the mystery of God's wholeness and presence in the cosmos through the power of his immanent Spirit. A positive outcome of the conversation with the new physics, then, is the opening up for theological reflection the vast mysterious universe from which, after billions of years of evolutionary history, we have emerged. We are only beginning to understand how 'finely tuned' the universe is for the emergence of life.

Thomas Berry, in his ecological theology, is very much concerned to restore the doctrine of creation to the centre of things.

He believes that recent advances in our understanding of nature add up to a new cosmic story which has spiritual implications for all of us. We form a crucial part of the story of the whole universe, which has come uniquely to self-consciousness in human beings. As agents of the universe's self-awareness, we ask, in its name, the great question of contingency, why there should be anything at all. Once we have grasped the awesome unity in diversity that is the cosmos it is possible to see the divine dimension. Berry points out that the cost of the scientific method is the giving up of the sense of the sacred in order to penetrate matter more fully. The danger is the loss of the sense that what is measured is more than its measurement.[40]

The twentieth century began in the long shadow cast by Charles Darwin, in a seemingly irreconcilable conflict between science and religion. The demise of religion was widely predicted; it did not happen. The three models of conflict, separation and interaction could be understood historically as stages in the journey of mutual understanding, from conflict to independence, to dialogue. Both science and religion arise out of the human desire to know, for the truth that lies at the heart of existence. Religion, according to John Haught, far from being in conflict with science, confirms the scientific enterprise. For him, the disinterested desire to know which is at the root of science 'finds its deepest confirmation in a religious interpretation of the universe'.[41] It does so, not by answering the specific questions of science, but by confirming the scientist's basic 'faith' in the limitless intelligibility and coherence of the real. The scientist's trust is grounded in a more fundamental frame of reference, in a God of love and promise who guarantees the cosmos' ultimate coherence and trustworthiness. According to Whitehead, 'The faith in the order of nature which made possible the growth of science is a particular example of a deeper faith.'[42] For Christians, 'this deeper faith' is most fully realised by the affirmation of faith in the compassionate and loving Father of Jesus Christ, creator and sustainer of the universe.

This is because they share a common origin in this fundamental human desire for the unity and coherence of all, knowing that science and theology, while acknowledging their diversity, can never be allowed to go their separate ways. At the end of the century the new dialogue is revealing, not only potentially new, exciting and fruitful areas of mutual interest, but a greater humility and a sensitivity to the scope and limitations of each.

NOTES

1. A. N. Whitehead, *Science and the Modern World*, New York, The Free Press, 1967, p.181.
2. Herbert Butterfield, *The Origins of Modern Science, 1300-1800*, New York, The Macmillan Company, 1951, p. viii.
3. Walter Kasper, *The God of Jesus Christ*, London, SCM Press, 1984, p.20.
4. Stephen Hawking, *A Brief History of Time*, London, Bantam Press, 1989, p.175.
5. In an interview in 'Masters of the Universe', BBC, 1989.
6. Paul Davies, *God and the New Physics*, New York, Simon and Schuster, 1983, viii-ix.
7. James Gleick, *The New York Times Magazine*, 4 January 1987.
8. The best examples are Ian Barbour, John Polkinghorne, Arthur Peacocke, Willem B. Drees, and Robert J. Russell.
9. See Ian Barbour, *Religion in an Age of Science*, San Francisco, Harper & Row, 1990; also John F. Haught, *Science and Religion: From Conflict to Conversation*, New Jersey, Paulist Press, 1995. My typology is a modification of both Barbour and Haught.
10. Carl Sagan, *Cosmos*, New York, Random House, 1980, p.4.
11. Walter Kasper, op. cit., p.26. It is interesting to note that Hawking's cosmology attempts to give to the universe characteristics often attributed to God, like eternal, timeless and necessary. See Willem B. Drees, *Beyond the Big Bang:*

Quantum Cosmologies and God, La Salle, Illinois, Open Court, 1990, pp. 69-75.

12. Arthur Peacocke, *God and the New Biology,* Gloucester, Mass., Peter Smith, 1994, p. 1.

13. Ian Barbour, *Religion in an Age of Science,* San Francisco, Harper & Row, 1990, pp. 7-8.

14. In 1981 the State of Arkansas sought to have 'creation science' given equal time with evolutionary theory in high school biology classes. The US Federal Supreme Court overturned the decision.

15. Ted Peters (ed.), *Cosmos as Creation,* Nashville, Abingdon Press, 1989, p.15.

16. Bryan Appleyard, *Understanding the Present: Science and the Soul of Modern Man,* New York, Doubleday, 1993, p.8. Appleyard has a Nietzschean view of science as subverting and belittling human values and spirituality.

17. Johann Wolfgang von Goethe, *Faust, Parts I and II,* ET Howard Brenton, London, Nick Hern Books, 1995, p. 25.

18. See John Hedley Brooke, *Science and Religion: Some historical Perspectives,* Cambridge, Cambridge University Press, 1991, p. 8ff. Brooke argues that the historical disputes between the Church and science have often been exaggerated by being removed from their social contexts.

19. Support for this position comes from Protestant neo-orthodoxy, from writers such as Karl Barth and Reinhold Niebuhr. From another direction a Wittgenstein 'language games' approach to theology would also fit in here.

20. See Langdon Gilkey, *Creationism on Trial: God and Evolution at Little Rock,* San Francisco, Harper & Row, 1985.

21. Rudolf Bultmann's uncritical acceptance of 'modernity', Newton's closed mechanical universe, in his demythologising of the New Testament is an example of the importation of a scientific theory into theology.

22. Stanley L. Jaki, *The Road of Science and the Ways of God,*

Chicago, Chicago University Press, 1978. Jaki argues that belief in creation and the Creator formed the bedrock on which science is founded. See David C. Lindberg and Ronald L. Numbers (eds.), *God and Nature: Historical Essays on the Encounter between Christianity and Science*, Berkeley, University of California Press, 1986. Also Nicholas Wolterstorff, *Reason within the Bounds of Religion*, Grand Rapids, William B. Eerdmans, 1976.

23. See Kitty Ferguson, *The Fire in the Equations: Science, Religion and the Search for God*, London, Bantam Press, 1994, p.8ff.

24. David Tracy, *Blessed Rage for Order*, New York, The Seabury Press, 1975, p.95.

25. Walter Kasper, op. cit., p.25.

26. Ian Barbour, *Religion in an Age of Science*, pp. 125-153.

27. Wolfhart Pannenberg, *Toward a Theology of Nature: Essays on Science and Faith*, Louisville, Westminster, John Knox Press, 1993, pp. 50-66. Pannenberg also wants to lead theology out of its self-imposed isolation in a renewed dialogue with science.

28. The search for consonance between theology and science is advocated by Ernan Mc Mullin, John Polkinghorne, Robert Russell and Ted Peters. See Ted Peters ed., *Cosmos and Creation: Theology and Science in Consonance*, Nashville, Abingdon Press, 1989.

29. Arthur Peacocke, 'The Challenge of Science to the Thinking Church', *Modern Believing*, Vol. xxxvi, no. 4, October 1995, p.17.

30. See J. Gleick, *Chaos: Making a New Science*, London, Heinemann, 1988.

31. See Thomas Berry, *The Dream of the Earth*, San Francisco, Sierra Club Books, 1988.

32. See Richard S. Westfall, *The Construction of Modern Science*, New York, Cambridge University Press, 1977, p. 30ff.

33. Michael J. Buckley SJ, *At the Origins of Modern Atheism,* New Haven, Yale University Press, 1987, p. 347ff. Buckley argues that modern atheism arose in part out of the physics and metaphysics of Isaac Newton and René Descartes respectively. Paradoxically, in their attempt to use mechanics and first philosophy as the foundation for the existence of God, they contributed to the rise for deism in the eighteenth century and eventually to the rise of atheism.

34. See Thomas Kuhn, *The Structure of Scientific Revolutions,* 2nd ed., Chicago, University of Chicago Press, 1970.

35. Jurgen Moltmann, *God in Creation: A New Theology of Creation and the Spirit of God,* San Francisco, Harper & Row, 1985, p.24.

36. Ian G. Barbour, *Religion in an Age of Science,* pp. 21, 33. This is particularly true in the quantum field where how we look changes what we find.

37. See Kitty Ferguson, op. cit., p. 84.

38. John Polkinghorne, *Science and Christian Belief,* London, SCM Press, 1992, p.7.

39. Moltmann, op. cit., p.31. For Moltmann, the emphasis on history in contemporary theology indicates a dualism that defines nature and history over against one another, exacerbating the ecological crisis.

40. See Thomas Berry, op. cit.; also Brian Swimme, *The Universe is a Green Dragon,* New York, Bear & Company, 1984.

41. John Haught, op. cit., p.22.

42. A. N. Whitehead, op. cit., p.18.

RELIGION AND CULTURE:
THE FREEDOM TO BE AN INDIVIDUAL

Eoin G. Cassidy

Anyone familiar with the changing face of Irish culture will realise that the emerging challenge to religious belief as this millennium draws to a close is religious indifference. To those born over fifty years ago this must seem an extraordinary state of affairs because, until very recently, religious belief seemed indelibly printed upon the very fabric of society. While one would not want to exaggerate the present extent of religious indifference in Ireland,[1] nevertheless many would suggest that the shape of Irish religious beliefs has already begun to merge with the pattern prevailing in the developed world. This emerging pattern is becoming most visible amongst the urban school population. Indeed, if the cultural antennas of religious educators in Ireland are sharply focused we are witnessing among our urban youth a far-reaching loss of religious experience. It is not only the ability of our young people to accept the content of the creed which is at stake, but their very ability to believe.

Religious indifference – a complex phenomenon
Religious indifference is a complex phenomenon because religious belief is complex. For instance, it could plausibly be argued that given the social character of Sunday Mass attendance in Ireland, there were, fifty years ago, nearly as many 'lapsed' atheists who went to Mass as there are 'practising' atheists today. Whatever about the accuracy of that observation it does alert us to the the dangers of identifying non-practice with unbelief. Religious belief has many dimensions – experiential, spiritual, doctrinal, moral and social as well as liturgical – and a person can be indifferent to one of these characteristics without

55

necessarily being indifferent to all the values or practices associated with religious belief. Religious indifference also has many dimensions and expresses itself in a variety of ways. Relative religious indifference is probably the most common form of religious indifference and reflects an à la carte approach to religion: as a result of a consumerist or instrumentalist attitude to life, religious belief is reduced to an assortment of isolated fragments. Then there is the absolute religious indifference which is indifference to religion *per se,* but not necessarily to secular values such as honesty, truthfulness, social justice, etc. This indifference can have its origins either in a belief in the self-sufficiency of science or in the perceived ineffectiveness of religion in addressing so many of the world's problems. Finally, we have the absolute indifference which proclaims that not only is there nothing worthy of belief but, more seriously, that there is no one to believe in: in most cases this stems from a pessimistic or fatalistic attitude to life – an experience of emptiness or a failure to find any meaning in life, attitudes which can be engendered by illness, loneliness, unemployment or the experience of rejection in a relationship.[2]

One of the most striking aspects of religious indifference is the newness of the phenomenon. If the acceptance of atheism has its origins in the relatively recent past, i.e. the culture of the Enlightenment in the late eighteenth century, then religious indifference is something very new. Significantly, the pre-1960 literature on the subject is sparse, with the exception of the rare – mainly French – publication. Furthermore, apart from being a recent cultural phenomenon, religious indifference is also almost exclusively confined to the 'developed' western world.

What, then, are the causal factors which have influenced the emergence of religious indifference in the western world? Theorists have not been slow to suggest causes. The list is impressive: secularism, pluralism, consumerism, scientific positivism, individualism and liberalism. However, we must distinguish between the creation of labels and the development of an understanding of the causes of something as multi-faceted as religious indifference: we must be especially conscious of the particularity of each local community or society.

For instance, the mose obvious particularity in Ireland is the link between Catholicism and nationalism which was such a dominant aspect of the Irish psyche until very recent times. Given the political desire of a significant proportion of Irish people in the late nineteenth and early twentieth century to liberate themselves from the ties created by the Act of Union, Catholicism became an essential badge of one type of Irishness. This link between nationalism and Catholicism was accentuated by the progressive decline of that other badge of distinctiveness, the Irish language. The historic need of the Irish people was to stress homogeneity, but times have changed: heterogeneity or pluralism is becoming the dominant emerging emphasis.[3]

This transformation of emphasis is partly a consequence of the natural journey of a nation and, more immediately, a consequence of specific and recent events. For example, the momentous and unexpectedly wide-reaching effects of the Republic of Ireland's entry into the European Economic Community in 1973 are only now beginning to reveal themselves. That event can truly be said to have marked the end of an era. No longer did southern Irish people feel the need to stress their separateness from Great Britain – in fact the opposite became the case. As members of the European Union the southern Irish have become partners, or at least, increasingly perceive themselves to be partners with the United Kingdom on a larger world stage. In this new context Catholicism is no longer the only badge or even the most appropriate symbol of national identity. When this factor is coupled with the seepage effect of the violence in Northern Ireland the consequence is that many southern Irish have become increasingly wary of an over-identification with either nationalism or Catholicism.

These and other themes could be developed at length in explaining the particularity of the Irish context. However, for present purposes, I wish to broaden the discussion of the roots of religious indifference beyond the specifically Irish context and to examine one of the themes of contemporary culture mentioned above, i.e. individualism. In what follows, I shall suggest that although individualism has contributed to a climate alien to the spread of Christianity, nevertheless, if the ideals associated with this phenomenon are sympathetically addressed, Christianity has the potential to offer a unique contribution to the furtherance of the contemporary quest of the individual.

Understanding individualism

Nothing has marked twentieth-century history so decisively as the cry 'Freedom'. Nearly every war in this century – against colonialism, fascism, poverty, communism, neo-colonialism – has been fought under this banner. In the so-called developed world it is no less evocative, but here it has its own particular colouring. The western world's cry is not just 'Freedom' but 'Freedom of the individual'. Powerful societal changes have prompted this cry: the advent of liberal democracy, the rise of a consumer and capitalist culture, the development of an urban and increasingly mobile, transient society. Intimations of these changes have been perceptible for the best part of two centuries but, until quite recently, many of these characteristics of con-temporary society were the exception rather than the rule, mar-ginal rather than central. This is certainly the case regarding the existence of liberal democracies. Even a mass consumer and cap-italist culture could hardly have been said to have pre-dated the first of the post-war consumer booms of the 1950s. An examina-tion of how these divergent societal changes combined, produces an interesting picture – one which reveals not only the cultural importantance of the notion of individual freedom but, more importantly, just how varied a notion it is.

Liberal democracy was founded on the desire to break free of authoritarian structures, to promote the autonomy of the human subject and to organise society in a manner that would accommodate difference or allow for the existence of a *de facto* pluralism. In particular, eighteenth-century Europe needed some structure of government which would ensure that the ravages occasioned by the century and more of conflict which followed the Reformation did not endlessly recur. In this context, liberal democracies sought and continue to seek to promote tolerance, pluralism and the rights of the individual.

From a very different perspective a capitalist and consumer culture also promotes an individualistic society. Precisely because it is premised on the idea of competition, a capitalist society must be an individualistic one, because market forces dictate that only the fittest will survive and that no matter what gloss one puts on it there are only two categories of being – winners and losers. In such a culture neighbours, friends and colleagues, whether at school, college or work are perceived, to a greater or lesser extent, as competitors or, at least, as potential competitors.

Again, from another perspective, this era, which is characterised by the ever-increasing development of an urban and transient society with a concomitant loss of a natural community, is perceived by many as rootless, anonymous and depersonalised. In such an environment, solitariness, even in the midst of many, is experienced in a way that would be alien and incomprehensible to a previous generation.

What is interesting is that there would seem to be three very different faces of individualism co-existing in contemporary western society and sometimes even in the one person: the tolerant liberal, the scrupulous or even unscrupulous competitor and the rootless solitary ego. Individualism as a theory expresses the way in which people see themselves in relation to society: simply stated, it asserts that one is first and foremost an individual rather than a social being. However, the above analysis suggests that this label of individualism can be understood in several very different ways. 'Freedom to be an individual' can mean freedom to be different, freedom to compete and freedom from any community or family ties.

Two of the better known philosophical and political theories of the present century have tended to mirror this scenario. The twentieth-century expression of existentialism which was founded on the ruins of early capitalism and the slaughter of trench warfare proclaimed the rebirth of a new solitary and heroic individual – a figure of Promethian stature who would challenge the gods of nationalism, fascism, capitalism, communism and all other 'isms'. It would dedicate itself to the struggle against those ideologues who tapped into the fears and insecurities caused by the loss of natural sources of community and attempted to transform individuals into cannon fodder for some larger cause. Another classic philosophical theory associated with the modern age is liberalism, which is the philosophical expression of liberal democracy and is based upon a commitment to a culture of tolerance and the protection or fostering of pluralism. In such a context individual rights are for the most part given priority over an ideal such as the common good.

One could scarcely find two more different philosophical map readings of culture – and both are classified under the rubric of individualism. Liberalism never was and could not be regarded today in anything like the same counter-cultural context as existentialism. The values enshrined in liberalism are those of liberty and equality – values which do not contradict those espoused by existentialism but which, nevertheless, have little in common with the latter's radical rejection of societal bonds.

These philosophies are relevant to any understanding of the changing horizon of religious belief in Ireland. In the name of the freedom and dignity of the individual, they both pose real, if very different, challenges to religious belief.

Individualism: An existentialist theme

With some notable exceptions, the culture that finds expression in what can loosely be called existentialism proclaimed that belief in God is incompatible with belief in individual freedom: humans are creators or creatures – either creators of meaning and value or creatures ordained to fulfil a plan which they have had no part in designing. A culture influenced by the atheistic strands of existentialism raises serious questions about the ethical character of religious belief. Religion is perceived as a philosophy of life not so much for the simple-minded as for the weak-willed. Religious belief is for those who lack the courage to be free, who lack the strength of character to embrace the world in all its nakedness. Furthermore, those who have been even vaguely influenced by an atheistic existentialist culture would perceive religion as attempting to undermine belief in the dignity of the individual. The struggle is to puncture the religious believers' arrogant assumption that, when faced with death, the atheist will succumb, before the promises of eternal life, or the fear of eternal damnation, and that the individual will thus be absorbed into the institution that is the Church.[4]

In this context, the challenge facing those concerned with making religion accessible to adults in the twenty-first century is to show, through a committed engagement with the concerns of the world, that religion is not a form of escapism. Just as importantly, they must challenge the assumption that a belief in God is incompatible with a belief in oneself as a creator of meaning and value. Finally, they must critique the myth of the free independent individual – a myth which in many ways could be said to define the twentieth century. As a descriptive model of human nature, it is one which all too frequently equates freedom with an ability to sever all familial or societal ties. Apart from the fact that this is simply not possible – and, therefore, in this scenario, freedom is, paradoxically, an impossible goal – it loses sight of the truth that there is no simple link between freedom and independence from all forms of community and tradition.

The religious believer who is a Christian proposes a different view of freedom, one that is found or received in and through the gift that is friendship or love. In the last analysis, relationship to family, friends and community can be seen as something which has to be kept in check, for fear that it would compromise freedom and independence, or else we can recognise that it is precisely the experience of rootedness in a community which frees the person to be an individual rather than being destructive of individuality. Clearly, it is only in this latter context that religious belief, Chrisianity in particular, can make any sense: Christianity proclaims that freedom is to be found in the experience of the community created by the dialectic of the love of God and the neighbour.

The importance of this issue can be seen in the context of the re-emergence in this century of extreme forms of nationalism leading to horrific examples of ethnic violence, for example against the Jews in Germany and the Muslims in Bosnia. Such outbursts of nationalist frenzy are a sobering reminder of the truth that individualism, which proclaims the dignity of the free solitary ego, is not a concept which has the ability to sustain the yearnings at the heart of human nature. Few can find lasting contentment in a rootless world. Individualism can never be anything more than skin deep because the yearning is always to belong, to be rooted in some community or tradition. When their natural community in an urban and transient society is lost or when their community seems threatened by internal or external forces, people become very vulnerable to manipulation by unscrupulous individuals. The task facing religious believers is to create communities which challenge the prevailing assumptions of nationalism and ethnicity, with their perversion and exploitation of the human need to belong. Twentieth-century European history shows how important and also how tragically difficult that challenge is for religious believers. It is, however, only by meeting that challenge, that conditions can be created where individuals can be truly free.

Individualism: An offshoot of a liberal culture

What about liberalism? Does it see religion as an uncomfortable partner in a world which values the individual? Ireland's very recent history seems to suggest that there is a strand in contemporary liberalism which regards religious belief – particularly that which is identified with Catholicism – as being hostile to the ideals associated with individual liberty, with individual rights being sacrificed on the altar of the common good or objective morality. At the very least, a suspicion exists that religions seek to have a particular moral code enshrined in law at the expense of a culture which promotes tolerance, pluralism and the liberty of the individual. There may even be the suspicion that the hidden agenda of all religions is something akin to a theocratic state, one which fosters religious hierarchies and oligarchies at the expense of a participative and egalitarian society. In this context many liberals would see liberal democracy and religion as uneasy bedfellows.[5]

It is ironic that the Catholic Church could be perceived as intrinsically hostile to individual liberty, considering that it is founded on the belief that all are created equal in the sight of God, and that all share the dignity of unique individuals, free and responsible before God. While taking care to avoid the relativist ethic of liberalism the greatest challenge facing Catholicism in the new millennium is unquestionably to devise structures which will allow these theological truths to find adequate expression in terms of the legitimate expectations of people who are used to living in a democratic culture. Although it can be cogently argued on theological grounds that the Church is not and never can be a democracy, there must be a sympathetic awareness of how people born into a democratic culture will perceive a hierarchical and centralised model of the Church. Democracies are, at least in principle, anti-hierarchical; they encourage participation in the democratic process and actively discourage passivity, to the extent that voting is compulsory in some countries in western Europe. While in practice equality may not be too evident in many democracies, a democratic culture is, nevertheless, one which places great emphasis on this ideal of equality. Where religions are perceived, rightly or wrongly, not to respect this ideal of a participative and egalitarian society, they are likely to be increasingly rejected by democratic culture. If the Church is to meet the demands of the new millennium it has no choice but to address the issue of how the structures of Church authority can be democratised.[6]

In the contemporary world, there is frequent and intense criticism of the Catholic Church's exercise of power as authoritarian. Paradoxically, a perceptive reader of history might argue convincingly that the Church is no more, and perhaps even less prone to authoritarianism today that at other times in its history. Furthermore, fifty years ago the Church in Ireland was certainly more hierarchically structured than it is today and arguably less sensitive, in practice, as distinct from theory, to the rights of the individual conscience. Yet, unlike today, few voices then criticised the Church as authoritarian. What has changed in the intervening period is society, rather than the Church.

Prescinding from the changing perception of the Catholic Church in Ireland over the last half century, reflection on the changing face of institutional structures across the whole spectrum of western society could be profitable. Fifty years ago a hierarchical structure in all facets of western society was the norm rather than the exception. Furthermore, the idea that membership of a workforce or society gave people the right to participate in decision-making would have been generally regarded as novel and dangerous. What was acceptable practice fifty years ago is no longer acceptable today. People are increasingly intolerant of any society or institution which is perceived as discouraging effective participation at all levels of decision-making. If the Catholic Church is to flourish in the new millennium, and, more importantly, if it is to act as an agent which frees people to be individuals it will have to respond creatively to this changed cultural environment. There is an urgent need to develop structures which encourage effective participation at all levels. In this regard, the Catholic Church has perhaps something to learn from some of the other Christian denominations.[7]

Individualism: A capitalist legacy

What of capitalism? Does that hidden and often unacknowledged philosophy of life, that philosophy for our contemporary urban and mobile society, challenge the religious values and beliefs associated with Christianity? Despite the apparently relaxed accommodation between Christianity and capitalism in the western world, there is little doubt that the radical, competitive strain of individualism which divides the world into winners and losers poses a far more fundamental threat to the value of Christianity than does either existentialism or liberalism. The values of capitalism are those of the market, where everything and everybody has a price and where everything and everybody has a shelf life. In this environment, the unconditional love of God or love of one's neighbour, to say nothing of the love of one's enemy, is an alien irrelevance. Despite the views of Karl Marx, there are many who would question whether, in a capitalist culture religion, in particular Christianity, will have a long shelf life.

Although capitalism purports to promote the freedom of the individual, there is, in a capitalist culture, an intense need for religion, if the true individual freedom is to be approached. Capitalism has prospered with the slogan 'freedom of the individual' and has used it to conquer and hold the high moral ground in its conflict with communism. Despite its effectiveness, the slogan is a mask which disguises the reality. In a capitalist culture people are free – but only if they have money. The poor have little freedom, the poor have few rights. It is only where capitalism has been tempered by socialist ideals that the poor have any rights or freedom worth talking about.

Another classic theme of capitalism is the ideal of being independent, self-sufficient. Capitalism decries the dependency or hand-out culture as it advocates the ideal of 'standing on one's own feet'. However, this form of independence is an impossibility, a misconception, a perversion of reality – and one which has the potential to marginalise large sections of society, such as the young, the old, the weak and the infirm.

Finally, it should be noted that for all its talk of freedom of choice a capitalist society offers very little real freedom, if the advertising industry is a good barometer of the capitalist value system. It is clear that what is offered by capitalism is a very one-dimensional vision of human fulfilment – one that focuses human freedom or choice almost exclusively on the attractiveness of consumer durables. We have the freedom to choose between different brand names but, given the pervasive power of the media, it is becoming increasingly difficult to choose a different value system from that offered by capitalism. In this context it is hard to speak with any confidence on the positive contribution of capitalism to the freedom of the individual. In short, capitalism both fosters a form of individualism that sacrifices the bonds of fraternity on the altar of competitiveness and ultimately destroys individual freedom, in any meaningful sense of the word, by demanding conformism to the dictates of consumerism.

The reality of capitalism and its underlying philosophy must be analysed if only to highlight the important contribution which religion could make to the promotion of the freedom of the individual. Christianity is founded on a value system which has little in common with a capitalist ethos. It is not simply that it proposes the ideal that the poor in spirit are blessed, rather it is that it contends that freedom is only to be found in the context of the experience of some solidarity with those who are on the margins of society. The ideal of 'minding one's own business' has little, if anything, in common with the role model proposed in the parable of the Good Samaritan. Christianity is thus challenged to critique capitalism in the cause of human emancipation. However, enormous difficulties face any philosophy of life which seeks to overturn or even modify the value system of capitalism. The writings of the contemporary 'critical theorists' offer ample evidence of the extent to which capitalism has successfully proposed itself as the only objective, rational system of social organisation. The logic of technical rationality is extremely hard to dent. Yet the challenge to do so has been taken up by communities in every corner of the world, many of whom have been influenced by the ideals associated with liberation theology. As Ireland also takes up the challenge, it may have much to learn from these communities as it joins them on the path towards a truer freedom of the individual – a freedom found in and through the experience of solidarity.[8]

Conclusion

It was the nineteenth-century Danish existentialist philosopher Søren Kierkegaard who rudely awakened his readers from over-reliance on the all too cosy crutch of institutional religion by reminding them that both Abraham and Jesus expressed their faith in moments of stark aloneness before God – Abraham with his son before the wooden pyre and Jesus on the wooden cross. It is in the spirit of Kierkegaard that we can recognise the nature of the true challenge facing the Church, namely, to highlight the unavoidability of individual freedom and responsibility. Christianity has unquestionably the potential to be the philosophy *par excellence* of the human subject. The new millennium needs to see a renewed commitment to preaching this message – one which tells us that not only are we free to be individuals but that it is only by accepting this freedom that we will be able to do justice to our dignity as human beings.

NOTES

1. For the most authoritative study of religious and moral values in Ireland see Christopher Whelan, *Values and Social Change in Ireland,* C. T. Whelan (ed.), 1994, pp. 7-44. This study, carried out under the auspices of the Economic and Social Research Institute and as part of the European Values Survey 1990, shows that the Irish profile, whether one examines Northern Ireland or the Republic (treated separately in the survey), is markedly different from that which is exhibited in any of the other European countries surveyed. The value of this work is enhanced by the fact that it offers a point of comparison with a similar survey carried out in 1981 and published under the title *Irish Values and Attitudes,* M. Fogarty *et al.* (eds.), 1984.

2. For a more detailed treatment of religious indifference see my 'Religious Indifference: An Atheism for today's world', in *Link-Up,* March, April, May/June, July, 1992, published by the Archdiocese of Dublin.

3. Robbie McVeigh has written an interesting article which throws light on this theme entitled 'Cherishing the Children of the Nation Unequally: Sectarianism in Ireland', in *Irish Society: Sociological Perspectives,* P. Clancy *et al.* (eds.), 1995, pp. 620-652.

4. Although published in 1976, John McQuarrie's *Existentialism* is still widely regarded as the best general introduction to the themes of existentialist philosophy.

5. This thesis is forcefully expressed by Desmond Clarke in his book *Church and State: Essays in political philosophy,* 1984. For an alternative view see Patrick Hannon's *Church and State: Morality and Law,* 1992. For an informative historical treatment of this theme see Tom Inglis, *Moral Monopoly: The*

Catholic Church in Modern Irish Society, 1987. See also Máire Nic Ghiolla Phádraig's article 'The Power of the Catholic Church in the Republic of Ireland', in *Irish Society: Sociological Perspectives,* P. Clancy *et al.* (eds.), 1995, pp. 593-619.

6. In a recent article entitled 'Structures of Authority' in *Authority in the Church,* Seán Mac Réamoinn (ed.), 1995, pp. 36-37, Bill Cosgrave underlines the importance of this task. In the following passage (at p. 37) he outlines his view of what is involved. 'While we would all agree that the Church is not formally a democracy, in the sense in which societies in the western world are nowadays democracies, there is every reason why, especially in the light of Vatican II, we should seek to develop in the Church what has been called an ethos of democracy. Such an ethos would espouse mutual respect, a readiness of members to make the common interest one's own, to listen to one another, and to ensure that all who are affected by a given decision are accorded a hearing. In a word, a democratic ethos calls for and involves the participation of all, dialogue and open communication at all levels, and participation in all decisions that affect one as a Church member.'

7. For a brief but illuminating treatment of alternative models of authority operative in some other Christian denominations see the articles by Catherine McGuinness, Gillian Kingston and Terence McCaughey, *Authority in the Church,* op. cit., pp. 67-92.

8. This is a theme which has been extensively developed in recent years. Among the Irish theologians who have made significant contributions one notes particularly Donal Dorr and Eamon Bredin. In particular see Donal Dorr, *Spirituality and Justice,* 1984, *Integral Spirituality,* 1990, and Eamon Bredin, *Disturbing the Peace,* 1985.

SELECT BIBLIOGRAPHY

Eamon Bredin, *Disturbing the Peace,* Dublin, The Columba Press, 1985.

Eoin G. Cassidy, 'Religious Indifference: An Atheism for today's world', *Link-Up,* Dublin, Audeon Press, 1992.

Patrick Clancy *et al.* (eds.) *Irish Society: Sociological Perspectives,* Dublin, Institute of Public Administration, 1995.

Desmond Clarke, *Church and State,* Cork, Cork University Press, 1984.

Donal Dorr, *Spirituality and Justice,* Dublin, Gill & Macmillan, 1984.

Donal Dorr, *Integral Spirituality,* Dublin, Gill & Macmillan, 1990.

Michael Fogarty *et al.* (eds.) *Irish Attitudes and Values,* Dublin, Dominican Publications, 1984.

Patrick Hannon, *Church and State: Morality and Law,* Dublin, Gill & Macmillan, 1992.

Tom Inglis, *Moral Monopoly: The Catholic Church in Modern Irish Society,* Dublin, Gill & Macmillan, 1987.

John McQuarrie, *Existentialism,* London, Penguin Books, 1976.

Seán Mac Réamoinn (ed.), *Authority in the Church,* Dublin, Columba Press, 1995.

Christopher T. Whelan (ed.) *Values and Social Change in Ireland,* Dublin, Gill & Macmillan, 1994.

POST-MODERNITY: FRIEND OR FOE?

Michael Paul Gallagher SJ

Post-modernity is more than merely a fashionable umbrella term: it seems a chameleon word that changes its colours depending on the philosophy of the user. For some authors post-modernity entails a radical critique and departure from what is meant by modernity, but others prefer to speak of 'late modernity', thus stressing that we are in a more advanced and problematic stage of much the same historical process. Anthony Giddens, the Cambridge sociologist, argues that we are a bit premature in terming our age post-modern. He prefers to speak of 'high modernity' (or 'radicalised modernity') because 'the consequences of modernity are becoming more radicalised and universalised than before'.[1] In particular he sees the zone of interpersonal trust or mutual self-disclosure as forced into unprecedented prominence because of the 'dispersals' or lack of anchors in contemporary culture.

Some weeks ago, when I was teaching a course at the Gregorian University in Rome, I asked the students to pool their insights on the characteristics of modernity and post-modernity. I filled the board with the answers. They came up with all the stock descriptions of modernity, valid so far as they go. Interestingly, they fell into two families, one to do with ideas and ideologies, and another focusing more on the individual self. For instance, among the more theoretical characteristics of modernity we listed: new trust in rationality, in science, in progress, in human control over nature and history, and a parallel distrust of tradition and authority, leading to a spirit of revolution in politics, and in the religious sphere the emergence of privatised faith and, ultimately, of 'modern' atheism. In the zone of the self, modernity seemed marked by a new primacy of individual dignity, personal rights, and autonomy of conscience, and therefore by a new sense of self-creative freedom in many fields.

An interesting trend emerged when we turned our attention to the characteristics of post-modernity. A whole series of question-marks were placed against some achievements of modernity, as contradictions long present in the modern enterprise came more sharply into focus. Did not the exciting novelties of science become frozen into a dehumanising of truth? Or the arrival of democracy sink into an anchorless liberalism? And so on. But then it became more than a matter of question-marks. Instead of having to write down new words on the board, all I had to do was draw a large X over various features of modernity. In fact, we ended up cancelling out all the non-individualist aspects of modernity. Thus, post-modernity looks with deep suspicion at an arrogant sense of reason, at scientism, at naive claims to progress, at insensitive dominance of the earth, at utopian perspectives on history. However, we did not put an X over the various forms of subjectivity fostered by modernity (nor over the related theme of rejection of authority). Instead, we added the term 'subjectivism', and discussed how in post-modernity the fate of the self deepens into a new loneliness and loss of connections. And yet one of the surprises of post-modernity seems to stem from this loneliness and shows itself in an openness to spiritual searching. On the religious front, post-modernity, at least in some of its tendencies, is much less sure of any black and white atheism.

In short the big claims of modernity have fallen under suspicion and have come to be largely rejected, but the 'turn to the subject' born with modernity has not only survived the transition but has become an even more crucial strand of our lived culture. It has given rise to a new sensibility that can be read either positively or negatively. According to one judgement we have fallen further into isolation, fragmentation and narcissism, where life is an indifferent game and individual options are merely aesthetic and provisional. But, according to another reading, the oft-maligned sense of self can be the source of our hope, because permanent hungers of the heart come to expression with new honesty and the quest for liberation and authenticity takes on a new humility. Even the sense of dispersal, according to this interpretation, rebounds into a new spiritual search for community and roots. Spirituality becomes not just a fashionable term but a real issue in this era beyond the oppressions of modernity.

Let us pursue this hunch by calling various experts to the witness-stand. In 1992 and 1993 two impressive books dealing with modernity were published. Although their approaches were very different, the American philosopher Louis Dupré (in *Passage to Modernity*) and the French sociologist Alain Touraine (in *Critique of Modernity*) agreed on one fundamental issue: that modernity involved a split between worlds, a disintegration of what had been a synthesis in the pre-modern situation. In Dupré's words, 'modernity is an event that has transformed the relation between the cosmos, its transcendent source, and its human interpreter'.[2] Very similar is Touraine's thesis that modernity defines itself by a growing separation of the objective or rational world from the world of subjectivity or individualism, rooted in an appeal to personal freedom.[3]

Putting them together, modernity causes a fragmentation of three horizons: the sense of self, the sense of truth and the sense of God. The self becomes lonely, self-conscious and withdrawn (and in literature the novel is born to mirror a new social class and replace the more public genre of drama). Truth, measured mainly with the instruments of empirical science, also withdraws into the sphere of the verifiable. God, as imagined by the defenders of faith in the seventeenth century and later, also retreats to theism and even deism: theologians become narrowly rational, forgetful of Christ, and leave the field of spirituality to sentiment.[4]

Before settling for this picture of multiple fracture as the core inheritance of modernity, another distinguished thinker should be called to the witness stand – Charles Taylor, the Canadian philosopher of cultural change. He might not disagree with the Dupré-Touraine convergence but he poses a usefully different question: what made this collapse of a previous coherence possible? Taylor shifts the drama to the world of sensibility, arguing that modern moral culture arrived when people no longer felt 'that the spiritual dimension of their lives was incomprehensible if one supposed there was no God'.[5] Why was it possible to imagine life without God? The answer involves both rationality and Romantic intuitions. The achievements of disengaged reason offered new grounds for self-dignity and for human autonomy, and the goodness of nature, as explored by creative imagination, offered a new secular spirituality. Thus Taylor, while echoing the insights of Dupré and Touraine about a new relationship to the cosmos brought about by a new rationality, brings in the crucial impact of the pre-Romantic valuing of sensibility as giving depth to the lonely self. Indeed, Taylor sees Romanticism as in large part a pre-modern form of expressivism, an effort to save humanity from the ravages of mere reason and the anonymous city – locating salvation immanently within the world of imagination and feeling.

Two poles of post-modernity

If all these forces were at work in modernity, not just as an ideology, but as an emerging sensibility, in a similar way we can identify two poles within post-modernity: it seems to reject the excessive certainties of modernity but not that second side of groping selfhood. Of course the most theoretical exponents of post-modernism voice scorn for humanism and the myth of the self, but they represent the more philosophical and nihilist camp within post-modernism (this militant wing I prefer to call post-modern*ism*). As distinct from these radical destroyers, post-modernity has also its more hopeful purifiers. Instead of delighting in dancing on the grave of modernity, these want to rescue it from its excesses and contradictions. From the point of view of religious faith, these less extreme post-moderns are new potential dialogue partners for theology. Not only have they something worthwhile to say about creating a non-ideological wavelength, but this less negative tendency within post-modernity seems in tune with some contemporary life-styles and searchings. In short, there are not only two branches of post-modernity but two levels where it can be found in our culture: in simple terms, one school is destructive, and the other constructive. The two levels are the post-modernist theory of intellectuals and the post-modernity implicitly lived in the new life-styles of today.

FACES OF POST-MODERNITY

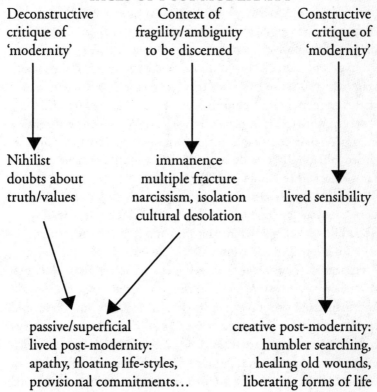

Deconstructive critique of 'modernity'	Context of fragility/ambiguity to be discerned	Constructive critique of 'modernity'

Nihilist doubts about truth/values

immanence
multiple fracture
narcissism, isolation
cultural desolation

lived sensibility

passive/superficial
lived post-modernity:
apathy, floating life-styles,
provisional commitments...

creative post-modernity:
humbler searching,
healing old wounds,
liberating forms of life

This is illustrated by the diagram on p. 75, which shows the opposite tendencies of deconstructive and 'constructive' post-modernity. Certainly we can find fragmentation, impotence and narcissism in the lived culture, but there is also a different searching beyond the old certitudes, including a new willingness to revisit the despised zones of the spiritual and the religious as roots of our healing. In the words of Charles Taylor, 'one has to see what is great in the culture of modernity, as well as what is shallow or dangerous'.[6] In this light post-modernity can mean retrieval of resources neglected through the lopsided triumph of modernity, old anchors like community, spirituality, and a new holism of human understanding.

In short if modernity involves separations of worlds, and if its lasting impact lies more in human sensibility than in ideas or ideologies, then post-modernity need not mean a further embracing of fragmentation, but a humbler recognition of wounds and wants. In this sense post-modernity can certainly be more friend than foe for religious commitment today. But before affirming that position too complacently, we have to face the opposing argument that post-modernity – although less ideologically hostile to religion than modernity – is in fact more apathetic and distant in its stance before possible religious faith.

Indeed there is a striking convergence between the independent analyses of Taylor, Touraine and Giddens on this issue. Together they suggest that the post-modern self suffers from a new isolation. The old supports of a cohesive society have almost disappeared. The anchors in religious belonging have lessened drastically for many people. In one way or another these three commentators propose a thesis of disintegration of a previous synthesis: that we live in the wake of multiple fracture, where the individual's various potential languages of searching are themselves cut off from one another. The sense of self, the sense of God, the sense of reality – all these are more radically divorced from each other than ever before in human history.

The convergence points towards a key insight: that post-modernity in its lived rather than theoretical forms manifests a lonely incapacity for roots. This loneliness shows itself in the fall-off from social visions and commitments concerning justice. It also shows itself in a loss of roots in the past, a kind of cultural amnesia. If this is valid as an emphasis, then judgmental and dismissive 'isms' are unworthy: it is not just a question of narcissism, hedonism, nihilism, post-materialism and so on. It is a question of suffering sensibility, of lostness, of handicapped searching within a culture that offers few lived connections with others or with roots of the past.

This picture seems at first to be one of cultural desolation, where the self finds only a desert situation, a wasteland absence of water. If faith, ever since we emerged from the easy inheritances of pre-modernity, has to be more a decision than before, a decision against the tide as in the early centuries of Christianity, then this landscape seems a formula for paralysis. Because of such little cultural support and such little attractiveness in the mediations of religion, faith decisions become uphill struggles, and when you add in the other pressures of trivial post-modernity in life-style, this faith dimension easily fades into unreality.

But everyone seems agreed, paradoxically, that a spiritual hunger is also stronger than in modernity, more acutely so because of the new cultural desolation and loneliness. Against the predictions of old-style sociologists of irreversible secularisation, post-modernity surprises us with the so-called 'return of the sacred'. But in what shape? Some years ago I was more positively disposed to the New Age tendencies, even if always suspicious of the New Age theories: at least there was some recognition of the spiritual dimension of life. But now I have hesitations about being too friendly even to the tendency. Just as sexuality was publicly suppressed in Victorian times, but found strange expressions in hidden pornography, a previously suppressed spirituality runs the risk of unwise forms. The hunger is real but with the cultural desolation and rootless amnesia, there is a danger of ending up with a floating spirituality that is radically different from the definiteness of Christian faith. New Age can even be a principal face of post-modern unbelief.

Although there is ambiguity there is also a new tone of openness. The theologian David Tracy has been concerning himself in recent years with the issue of post-modernity, stressing that it represents both a cultural and a theological category. He seems in agreement with the emerging consensus that post-modernity is a new sensibility, more open to religious horizons than during the long reign of modernity. He praises the key achievements of modernity – the philosophical maturity born from the crisis of the scientific revolution, the 'bracing honesty of an historical consciousness', the liberating aspects of the democratic ideal – and yet he discerns a dangerous levelling and pride within modernity, a 'drive to sameness, the modern western scientific, technological, democratic culture that is culture and history', the arrogance of modern liberalism that never says out loud but implies that 'western culture *is* culture'.[7]

According to Tracy, it becomes possible to stress again the crucial frontiers between theology and spirituality. Modernity tended to reduce everything to external 'religion' or even to deism. Post-modernity is more open to the prophetic, cosmological, mystical or participative dimensions of religious experience. A post-modern spirituality can be born that does justice both to the core relationship of faith, the radical concreteness of Christ and his prophetic challenges for our broken worlds, and values equally the wise shyness of an apophatic theology, reticent to explain its mystery, or to name it too neatly and, above all, healthily suspicious of cheap words.

Towards a balance sheet
Perhaps there is a tendency to be too hard on modernity and too rosy about the more holistic sensitivity of post-modernity. Be

that as it may, the case for a positive view of this new sensibility is based on a double claim to heal some of the human wounds of modernity and to reopen neglected wavelengths of exploration. Where modernity left us lonely and without purpose, post-modernity seeks to expand the set of relationships, cosmic and communitarian, and to reopen the conversation about the ultimate goal of life.

According to these more favourable interpretations post-modernity is characterised by radical new sensitivities on three fronts: ecology, feminism, and the return of spirituality. Indeed the three areas are deeply connected; they are rooted in a realisation that our history has suppressed something precious which now needs liberation. Modernity was exploitative of the earth and of peoples, forgetful of women and of the feminine in each person, and it forced the spiritual dimension of life to retreat to the poetic and the private. If so, post-modernity proposes a series of openings. As yet it may be more sure of its negatives than its positives. And yet these three cultural presences, which were not so strongly felt even a generation ago, together represent a major shift in sensibility.

In my browsing through the literature of post-modernity and theology, I have found that Spanish-language theologians seem to offer the most positive readings of this new sensibility. José María Mardones, Luis González-Carvajal or Alejandro Llano single out several zones of purification and hope for faith:[8] the return of attention to religious experience, an area despised as illusory by modernity; a healthy distance between religion and manipulative or totalising power systems, as fostered especially by liberation theologies; prophetic critique of the idols of theism (a first cousin of modernity) and of rationally packaged versions of God; more positively, a quest for more adequate wavelengths before divine mystery, shown in retrievals of negative or narrative theology; renewal in the aesthetic or festive or contemplative aspects of faith (even von Balthasar can be seen as post-modern in a certain sense); a Christianity that faces the challenge of differentness of cultures, overcoming modernity's suppression of this diversity; and while there are new risks of a narcissistic and 'light' religiousness within trivial post-modernity, there is the opposite tendency to trust the fragment and forge a pilgrim and patient spirituality of option for the poor. Llano speaks of post-modernity as returning to an analogical way of thinking as a non-rationalist and gradualist approach to meaning, and in this he sees hope for linking *praxis* and *poeisis,* which had been long polarised in classical modernity. One finds something of the same 'friendly' diagnosis in Elizabeth Johnson who sees 'post-modern consciousness' as aware of 'the fragility of the human project' and yet prizing 'essential connectedness' and the 'importance of community'.[9]

Conclusion

Do we need yet another distinction, perhaps, between passive and creative post-modernity (as indicated at the bottom of the diagram)? Passive would point to the drifting nature of contemporary life-styles – what can be described as the 'alienated immediacy' and fret of consumerist existence (Enzo Bianchi), or as the cultivated cynicism that reigns in sophisticated circles (and which echoes the more conscious negativity of post-modern*ism*). Whereas this passive post-modernity seems in continuity with the voids of modernity and, in terms of religion, is a form of apathy and distance even from the hungers of faith, a more critical post-modernity questions all that long amnesia. It seeks to forge a new language of living for today. It reopens doors locked or at least neglected by modernity. It hopes to find ways of healing our inherited forms of loneliness – all those separations of self from society, or reason from feeling, or science from religion, or man from woman, or theology from spirituality, or individual depth from embracing the struggles of history. Put like this, it could seem another cultural dream like Romanticism, another utopian agenda, doomed to disappointment. But there is a certain saving grace of humility at the heart of this post-modernity that starts small, goes one step at a time, and values the limited horizon of the possible. With this qualification, disappointments can perhaps be avoided, because at its best it seeks to discern our needed liberations if we are not to suffer from new oppressions of our humanity and our imagination.

Besides, we need a post-modernity of our own Christian making, an energetic seizing of the moment. It is not a question of watching the signs of the times, hoping passively for a change in the weather, but rather of seeing that this humbler moment after modernity is itself already a friendly moment for creative embodiment of the Christian vision. Possibilities open up for a recovery of a more genuine sense of self after identifying the damage of false individuality as proposed by hard modernity. Parallel possibilities open up to link this new search of the self with communitarian and spiritual horizons – in ways that have not been culturally credible for centuries. When the self is less lonely, when the culture finds its shared language of community at the local and world levels of justice, when theology finds new ground with spirituality, then we are talking about a new sensibility that is far from vague. It is a convergence of hungers and of potentials that is fresh and friendly for a new language of faith. In this light, critical and creative post-modernity is not only the friend of Christian faith, but a cultural wavelength in which faith can make itself liveable and credible for today.

NOTES

1. *The Consequences of Modernity,* Cambridge, Polity Press, 1990, p. 3.
2. Louis Dupré, *Passage to Modernity,* New Haven, Yale University Press, 1993, p. 249.
3. Alain Touraine, *Critique of Modernity,* Oxford, Blackwell, 1995, preface.

4. See Michael J. Buckley, *At the Origins of Modern Atheism*, New Haven, Yale University Press, 1987.
5. *Sources of the Self: the making of modern identity*, Cambridge, Harvard University Press, 1989, p. 310.
6. *The Ethics of Authenticity*, Cambridge, Harvard University Press, 1991, p. 120.
7. David Tracy, 'Theology and the Many Faces of Post-modernity', *Theology Today*, 1994, Vol. 51, pp. 104-114; quotations from pp. 104-107.
8. See José María Mardones, *El desafío de la postmodernidad al cristianismo*, Santander, Sal Terrae, 1988; Luis González-Carvajal, *Ideas y creecias de hombre actual*, Santander, Sal Terrae, 1991; Alejandro Llano, *La nouva sensibilità: il positivo della società postmoderna*, Milan, Ares, 1995.
9. Elizabeth Johnson, 'Between the Times: religious life and the postmodern experience of God', *Review for Religious*, 1994, Vol. 53, pp. 6-28; quotations from pp. 18-19.

IRISH CATHOLICS – A PEOPLE FORMED BY RITUAL

Michael Drumm

The dialogue of faith and culture is a particularly pertinent one for contemporary Christian believers in Ireland. In this dialogue insufficient attention has been paid to historical studies despite the fact that outstanding work is now available concerning the evolution of the Christian Churches in Ireland, particularly in the nineteenth century. In this paper I would like to analyse the overwhelming importance of the Great Hunger of 1845-48 in shaping the religious consciousness of Irish Catholics. Only when due weight is given to the historical and theological consequences of this famine can an adequate interpretation of many characteristics of the contemporary dialogue of faith and culture in the Irish context be provided. These include the implications of the coincidence of industrialisation in Ireland with the Second Vatican Council, the historical mistrust so characteristic of relations between Protestants and Catholics, the incredibly slow emergence of enlightenment consciousness, the attachment of Irish Catholics to religious-based ritual, the explosion in the numbers of clergy and religious from 1850 to 1970, the missionary outreach and the dominance of educational concerns in Church-State relations. These varied issues find a focus in one question: Why, for one hundred years, did Irish Catholics both at home and in the diaspora maintain a level of church attendance which seems unparalleled in history? The really significant question is not why Irish Catholics are now showing signs of falling levels of attendance more in keeping with the norm in similar countries, but rather why such levels of practice ever emerged in the first place.

In order to answer this question the effects of the Great

Hunger of 1845-48 on the religious consciousness of Irish Catholics must be analysed. Prior to the Famine Irish Catholicism could be described as a traditional religion blending folk customs with Christian orthodoxy. Other adjectives such as 'folk' or 'popular' could be used to describe it but these terms give rise to pejorative interpretations. When people speak of popular, folk religion they often intend to contrast this with mainstream monotheistic 'true' religion, the latter functioning as a purifier of the insidious idolatry of the former. When I refer to traditional religion I mean the matrix of beliefs, practices, rituals and customs that constitute a living incarnate religion which functions in a very practical way as an interpretative model of human existence and brings together in an apparently 'unholy alliance' the residue of archaic fertility rites, land-based rituals, orthodox Christian beliefs and a broad notion of the sacramentality of life. There is much in the traditional practices of Irish Catholics that has not been integrated into any coherent theological framework; fairy forts, holy wells, bonfire nights, ghost stories, pilgrimages, patterns and wakes have constituted rich data for folklorists, artists and anthropologists but have been largely ignored by Irish theologians. Yet it was these very customs which defined the religious outlook of Irish Catholics for centuries.

There are then two questions that are particularly apposite in the context of the dialogue of faith and culture in Ireland: What value should be placed on the many expressions of traditional religion amongst Irish Catholics? How should the very strong attachment of Irish Catholics to chapel-centred rituals over the last one hundred and fifty years be interpreted?

Pre-Famine religious expression

The Celtic year revolved around four great feasts: 1 February, Imbolg, with the start of tilling, the birth of lambs, the return of fishermen to the sea and varied efforts to foretell the weather for the coming summer; 1 May, Bealtaine, when cattle returned to pasture accompanied by all sorts of ritual and prayers of protection; 1 August, Lughnasa, the celebration of the first fruits of the harvest with people gathering at heights and wells for feasting and games; fairs and horse races were common; 1 November, Samhain, the festival of the disappearing sun and the other world. Strange powers and people were easily accessible at this time of the year. These great feasts were in large part integrated into the lives of Irish Christians but the violent iconoclastic forces unleashed by the Reformation led to a sustained attack upon this strange Irish mix of pagan culture and Christian belief. Similarly the Counter-Reformation sought to restructure the Catholic Church through purging many traditional practices in the embrace of an essentially clerical ecclesial vision. Yet, despite the best efforts of the various Christian denominations and the state apparatus the people clung to their archaic ritual celebrations which probably dated back more than two thousand years. The Famine was to change all that.

It is interesting that the retrieval of these traditions in contemporary Irish consciousness is found in the work of poets, artists and playwrights and seems almost completely absent in the work of theologians. Seamus Heaney's *Station Island* [1] and Brian Friel's *Dancing at Lughnasa* [2] are outstanding contributions to re-imagining traditional Irish religion – these authors go to the margins of their own experience in order to revisit the liminal space often inhabited by their forebears. Irish Churches and theologians have been slow to visit these well-springs, mainly because of the events of the 1840s and their repercussions.

Religion and the Famine

Anglican evangelicals and the majority of Catholic priests had one aim in common in the first half of the nineteenth century – to convert the people, with their predilection for pagan rites, to true Christianity. But it was the Famine that changed everything and facilitated the emergence of that pious individualism which is so characteristic of late nineteenth- and twentieth-century Christianity. Between 1845-48 the world of the poor Irish peasants ruptured and died; there were no new potatoes to celebrate at Lughnasa and the ancient traditions must have seemed empty in the face of such a calamity. As, centuries previously, the Black Death had changed the religious consciousness of Europe, so the religious mind and heart of the Irish peasantry would be transformed. It is in this sense that it is probably true to speak of contemporary Irish Catholicism as a post-Famine phenomenon. There was a relentless attack on traditional rituals and, as Eamon Duffy comments on the similar iconoclasm of the Reformation in England, 'the attack on them was an effort to redefine the boundaries of human community and, in an act of exorcism, to limit the claims of the past, and the people of the past, on the people of the present'.[3] The cataclysm of the Great Hunger was just such a possibility for exorcism and there was no shortage of Protestant and Catholic exorcists.

The iconoclasm of Protestant evangelicals with regard to the Irish folk traditions was clear-cut. Here was a quasi-pagan people placating superstitious gods and seeking to earn salvation. The comments of Rev. Henry M'Manus, a Presbyterian missionary who was in the Joyce country of the Maumturk mountains in July 1841, are typical. Having described the celebration of a Mass at the Lughnasa festival he goes on to say:

> This worship was followed by a sudden transition, characteristic in all ages, of the religion which man himself originates, and which he loves. Amusement became the order of the day. The pipers struck up their merry tunes in the tents, and the dancing began ... Bread and cakes were abundantly supplied by peddlers and whiskey flowed on all sides. Under such circumstances we may conceive the uproarious hilarity of an excitable people. Nor did it all cease till the Sabbath sun sought the western wave.[4]

Suggestions of cultural superiority were common amongst Protestant commentators, yet what was really significant was the perceived effort to convert the Irish poor through what came to be known as the 'New Reformation'. Relationships between Anglicans and Catholics deteriorated noticeably from the 1820s onwards; Catholics in Ireland believed that a new proselytising zeal was evident amongst Anglican evangelicals whilst a resurgent Catholicism in England sowed fear in the hearts of many Irish Protestants. These tensions ultimately found their focus in the Famine controversy over 'souperism', the claim that Anglican evangelicals distributed soup to impoverished Catholics on condition that they converted to Anglicanism and sent their children to what was effectively the equivalent of Sunday School. People who 'took the soup' became known as 'soupers'; later Irish Catholic tradition used this term pejoratively to identify those who had apostasised and to highlight the great Catholic triumph in convincing most adherents not to 'take the soup'. That some Anglican evangelicals indulged in this grotesque form of proselytism is unquestionably true, that most Irish Anglican pastors abhorred the practice is equally true.[5] The guilty included Thomas Plunkett, Bishop of the united dioceses of Tuam, Killala and Achonry, Alexander R.C. Dallas, founder of the Society for Irish Church Missions, and Edward Nangle, who set up a Protestant colony in Achill. Their actions, particularly in County Mayo, were abhorrent and were well summarised by Dallas himself when he wrote that his movement

> ...was nurtured in blood, the awful famine of 1847, with its attendant horrors in 1848 worked wonderfully for its development. Thus it might almost be said that the movement gave a character to the famine rather than the famine characterised the movement.[6]

Understandably Catholic leaders responded aggressively to

what they perceived to be a Second Reformation; Tobias Kirby advised the bishops 'to repress any efforts of the Protestants who give the poor a morsel of bread with one hand and kill their immortal souls with the other'.[7] As before, a Reformation would be met head-on with a Counter-Reformation.

The leader of this Counter-Reformation was Paul Cullen. Donal A. Kerr comments that 'for Cullen, countering Protestant proselytism was a priority and his hatred of it is crucial to an understanding of his policy in his early years in Ireland'.[8] The effect of Cullen on the post-Famine Church is so enormous that some have termed it the 'Cullenisation' of Irish Catholicism. In a famous article Emmet Larkin describes the changes that occurred as amounting to a 'devotional revolution'.[9] The most powerful expression of this 'revolution' was probably found in the parish mission which seemed to make an almost indelible mark on participants. The missioners – Vincentians, Redemptorists, Jesuits – came from abroad to inculcate renewed theological emphases:

> ...for instance, the decided dualism of salvation theology, the heavy reliance on sacrament and sacramental to under-pin evangelisation, the primacy of confession in pastoral strategy, the defensive stance of ecclesiology, the weaning of the people from an over-reliance on elements of folk religion to a chapel-centred practice of faith.[10]

The latter was all-important because, as a result of the suppression of the monasteries and Church buildings under Henry VIII in the mid-sixteenth century and the continuing legal hostility to Catholicism right through to the early nineteenth century, there was a paucity of church buildings in Ireland. The first half of the nineteenth century saw an explosion in the building of chapels with maybe as many as one thousand new constructions. The key pastoral goal of Archbishop Cullen was to turn Irish Catholics into a church-going population; he achieved this through insisting that Mass be offered only in chapels, so station Masses were suppressed; through removing corpses from homes to chapels, so funeral wakes were undermined; and by suppressing many of the traditional practices and replacing them with chapel-centred imports such as 'forty hours, perpetual adoration, novenas, blessed altars, Via Crucis, benediction, vespers, devotion to the Sacred Heart and the Immaculate Conception, jubilees, triduums, pilgrimages, shrines, processions and retreats'.[11] Groups emerged to promote participation in these exercises: confraternities, sodalities, Children of Mary, altar and temperance societies. 'These public exercises were also reinforced by the use of devotional tools and aids: beads, scapulars, medals, missals, prayer books, catechisms and holy pictures.'[12] By 1870 the Cullen reforms were triumphant, the census returns of 1861 proved that the efforts of Protestant proselytisers were essentially a failure and the 'great mass of the Irish people became practising Catholics, which they have uniquely and essentially remained both at home and abroad down to the present day'.[13] One of the most interesting aspects of this zealous reform was that Irish clergy whether in Belmullet or Brooklyn, Cricklewood or Cape Town, Limerick or Lagos, pursued the same pastoral strategies from the 1850s until the 1960s.

As usual this revolution/evolution was iconophile with regard to its new practices and radically iconoclast concerning folk traditions. Pilgrimages to holy wells, even at Lughnasa, continued but they had nothing to do with the celebration of first fruits; commonly they were portrayed as temperance gatherings, the rounds were made but there were no festivities. The ancient ascetic spirit so well manifested on Croagh Patrick and Lough Derg became overlaid with sexual overtones; it wasn't difficult to link sexual behaviour, guilt, sin and death in the minds of these people for, all too obviously, there had been too many mouths to feed. The spirit of the people was broken by the Famine and the new spirituality assumed the high moral ground of the respectable middle class, rejecting the raucous religion of an earlier time in the embrace of individual rigour, personal scrupulosity and sexual abstinence. Nowhere was this spirit more manifest than in the great symbol of post-Famine Irish Catholicism – the sacrament of confession.

It is important to note that many historians disagree with Larkin's analysis. They prefer to speak of a 'devotional evolution' rather than a 'devotional revolution', as it took almost three centuries for a truly tridentine Church to be established in Ireland.[14] The core of the tridentine counter-reformation was the parish priest in his church building providing frequent access to the sacraments. By definition this could not be the case in Ireland since the suppression of the monasteries under Henry VIII and the effective ban on Catholic Church building right through to the end of the eighteenth century. As a result the Catholicism practised by the Irish peasants inevitably revolved around their homes and townlands rather than chapels. But we should be careful not to dismiss this form of religious expression as effectively non-Catholic. Thomas G. McGrath comments:

> Do we acknowledge a valid role for popular religion or do we look on the venerable devotions of popular religion with their now seemingly incongruous mixture of the sacred and the profane as merely superstitions or as evidence that these people were not practising Catholics at all? To do so would be a condescending dismissal and a dangerous misreading of the vibrant heritage of Irish Catholicism.[15]

Indeed it would and Larkin must be faulted in so far as he does so. Yet the fact remains that we must not underestimate the significance of the Famine in forging a new religious consciousness. Kerr comments:

The cluster of beliefs and practices that constituted the religion of the poorer peasants, in addition to such central Catholic devotions as the sacraments, the rosary, fasting and daily prayers, also included devotions connected with patterns, pilgrimages, holy wells, wakes and charms. Many of these came under attack, as a reforming Church opposed them as either superstitious or providing the occasion for insobriety, immorality, or other abuses. The Famine dealt them a devastating blow, for it bore heaviest on the labouring and cottier classes. Thenceforth, religious practices became more 'orthodox' and the quickening pace at which this took place wrought a rapid change in Irish devotional life.[16]

And yet the change was not complete, the exorcism failed to banish all the ancient archetypes. Despite the unleashing of massive iconoclastic forces in the midst of a society in disarray, where death and emigration stalked the land and the language of the people faced near terminal decline, this effort to redefine the boundaries of human community by banishing so many traditions could not ultimately succeed as it failed to give due weight to the imagination and its capacity to revisit these ancient wellsprings. Cullen's reforms crept westwards through the country slowly but surely, yet they never managed to extinguish the old traditions completely and so, one hundred and fifty years later, we can inhabit the same spaces as our forebears at station Masses, funeral wakes, patterns, holy wells and pilgrimages. But we revisit these spaces with a post-Famine consciousness.

Given the enormity of the forces unleashed in Ireland in the middle of the nineteenth century we should be slow to underestimate their effects on the consciousness of Irish Catholics. I would like to look briefly at three such effects.

1. *Suppressing the memory*

One of the key insights of contemporary psychology is that people suppress the memory of great traumas in their individual lives. Similarly Irish people suppressed the memory of the Great Famine. When we begin to delve into the enormity of the horror that was unleashed this is easy to understand. The Irish Famine is one of the great disasters of peacetime history. In the aftermath of famine there are no good stories to tell; rather the chances are that the main stories are of neglect, cheating, stealing, gaining on the backs of others and the ultimate horror – cannibalism. This is not the stuff of songs and fireside storytelling. In famine it is impossible to identify the enemy and so heroism is difficult to describe: it is easy enough to identify and laud the hero in the face of colonial occupation but what is heroism in the face of blight? Who were the heroes – those who died? Those who emigrated? Those who survived at home?

The latter group gained as a result of the Famine and we can legitimately speak of a survivor complex. It seems almost too obvious to remark upon but it is worth reflecting on the fact that the people who now live in Ireland are the descendants of those who survived the horror of famine; the majority of their forebears did not die or emigrate. In reality the gains in the medium term for those who survived were hugely significant economically, socially and politically. It seems plausible to surmise that they might indeed repress the memory of the Great Hunger and in this their behaviour is clearly distinct from the Irish of the diaspora. Folklore traditions amongst the native Irish relating to the Famine are scarce whereas it remained one of the great themes in the lives of the Irish of the diaspora. Here's a simple example: ask Irish Catholics living in Ireland to analyse the historical causes of the troubles since 1969 and they will speak of plantations and Cromwell; ask the same question in Irish Catholic working-class areas of Liverpool or Boston and one will almost invariably hear of the Famine. The ultimate demonstration of suppressing the memory was the centenary years of 1945-48 when the neophyte state all but ignored the events of one hundred years earlier.

Why do we now recall the Famine one hundred and fifty years later? As ever historical distance has opened up more space to reflect. Poets,[17] dramatists[18] and historians have given us language, images and analysis to think through the horror. Missionaries have encountered famine anew and their contemporary experience has retrieved a long-lost memory in the Irish psyche. It is imperative that we the descendants of the survivors now remember what happened. The best way to do so is through ritual which allows us to celebrate rather than just study the past. Imagine the significance of a small community gathering to honour an unmarked mass grave, to admit the pain of history, to pray for responsible leadership, to hope for justice and to lay to rest finally those who died such terrible deaths. We need to remember so that we can legitimately forget. There are places in the land and places in the soul where we can remember; having visited these places we can, indeed we probably must, legitimately forget.

2. *Surviving the consequences*

People and institutions adapt and change in the midst of overwhelming catastrophes. The Irish Catholic Church was rocked to its very core by the events of the 1840s and not least by the widely held belief that Anglicans and Presbyterians had used the tragedy for their own purposes. The Catholic Church under Cullen's leadership and with the outstanding contribution of the new religious orders responded aggressively. Education and health care provision became key pastoral goals in Irish Catholic communities throughout the world as people sought to protect themselves against future horrors. Irish Catholics began to build – churches, presbyteries, hospitals, schools, – and for a people bereft of buildings for centuries these new constructions became an important symbol of their faith; even today we hear the complaint that Irish clergy are preoccupied with church buildings to the neglect of more important pastoral issues. But we shouldn't lightly dismiss the psychological importance of these new buildings that sprouted up all over the country in the latter part of the last century; at least one Catholic would live in a house to vie with the local landlord, and so the parish priest's house was a rather large construction for a single, celibate man.

The consequences of the Famine were evident in all spheres of Irish life but probably nowhere more clearly than in attitudes towards sexuality. After the Famine people married later in life, many never married at all; the Catholic Church preached a message of temperance and sexual abstinence and, as was noted earlier, the newly emerging Catholic middle class rejected the raucous religious expression of an earlier age in the embrace of personal scrupulosity, individual ambition and religious rigour. The latter was facilitated by frequent recourse to the sacrament of confession whilst the dominance of Victorian values in a wider context reinforced an atmosphere of sexual repression. In the aftermath of terrible famine it is not difficult to link sexual expression and guilt; celibacy and sexual abstinence would have emerged as socio-economic as well as religious values. Sexual experience and guilt feelings appear to be linked in many different ways but one must surely regret the oppressive ethos of sexual repression so characteristic of post-Famine Irish life.

3. *Characterising relationships*
Relationships between Irish Catholics and Protestants have always been fraught but probably hit their lowest ebb in the immediate aftermath of the Famine. There have been sectarian riots on the streets of Belfast in every decade since the 1840s, the claims concerning 'souperism' poisoned relationships in many local communities, and it is only since the 1960s that a real dialogue has commenced. There is deep suspicion between the Christian communities in Ireland over land, nationality and colonialism; the wounds of history are deep. The imagination

still bears the scars of the famine that was endured, the land that was fought over and the language that was suppressed. Famine, land, language – are there any greater forces for forming the imagination? It is hardly surprising that feelings of inferiority, peasantry and pain are so much a part of Irish Catholic consciousness. The great danger with an inferiority complex is that it causes people to withdraw into a ghetto in their own smugly secure certainties concerning the hostile world outside. Unquestionably Irish Catholicism gave way to this temptation so that as late as the 1950s the best minds of the Irish Catholic Church were dealing with questions such as attendance at services in Protestant churches, State regulations concerning dances and endless minutiae concerning liturgical rubrics.[19]

But there is another relationship that might prove even more important in the longer run – the relationship of Irish Catholics to the enlightenment consciousness of the modern world. The conventional wisdom of the liberal media/academic establishment in contemporary Ireland is that Irish Catholics were held in bondage for centuries by an oppressive Church and that only with open access to education since the 1960s have people begun to escape the clutches of this all-powerful institution. I believe this form of analysis to be fundamentally flawed. As a simple hypothesis which explains everything that needs to be explained it is very attractive but such all-embracing hypotheses are almost invariably false. What alternative explanation might be offered? I have suggested that we have failed to give sufficient weight to the effect of the Great Hunger of the 1840s on Irish Catholic consciousness. The enlightenment did not influence Irish Catholics because the Famine had turned their hearts and minds in a different direction – not towards the rights of the individual, freedom of enquiry, respect for the emerging sciences and progress; but towards survival, tenant rights, emigration and fear of what life might hold. It took generations to come to terms with these issues. As a result there is an extraordinary coincidence in Ireland

in the 1960s of modernity (in terms of the beginning of industrialisation, urbanisation and secularisation) with the Second
Vatican Council. Just as modernity was beginning to doubt its
own values both Ireland and the Catholic Church were embracing it for the first time. For Irish Catholics it was a time of overwhelming change; there was the crucial call to inculturate the
faith in a truly modern way so that believers could articulate their
faith for a new, emerging world.[20] This must remain the key pastoral priority for the Irish Catholic Church and several writers in
this volume address this precise issue. I have attempted to
demonstrate that if we ignore the historical experience of famine
in Ireland then we are likely to draw many mistaken conclusions
about the nature of Irish Catholicism.

Conclusion

The inter-relationship of faith and culture is, from a theological
perspective, an issue of inculturation – of how Christian belief is
articulated and incarnated in a particular culture. In the Irish
context we must remember that the dialogue of faith and culture
goes back about fifteen hundred years and that it endured one of
the great peacetime calamities in the middle of the last century.
One should not reduce this dialogue to simply a matter of how
Irish Catholicism might interact with the enlightenment. Rather
we might bring forth many riches from our past to help us incarnate the faith in a post-modern context. We could look again at
the emphasis on communal rituals rather than just the individual
subject's search for meaning; at the interaction of Christian and
pagan motifs; at the celebration of the earth; at the encounter
with the numinous and otherness in many of our traditions. This
is already happening in what is termed 'celtic spirituality', but we
should be aware that this spirituality is filtered through the historical experience of Irish Catholics; there is no ahistorical access
to such a spirituality.

As we attempt to decipher our past we must be careful not to dismiss the religious experience of our forebears as little more than pre-modern ritualism. A poor and broken people are always iconophile for they have little to hold on to and even less to explain what is happening. The iconoclasm of the well-fed stomach should at least hesitate in its theological judgements. Hunger stalked the land of Ireland many times in the nineteenth century; most shockingly of all it revisited the people of Connaught thirty years after the Great Hunger in the late 1870s. In 1879 the poor of Mayo were in a wretched state, there was nothing to celebrate around Lughnasa as the potato crop failed and, on 21 August, several people claimed to see a Marian apparition on the gable wall of the church in Knock. Michael Davitt's land war was about to begin and the word 'boycott' would soon enter the English language. Yet again the complex iconography of the Irish was expressing itself.

Great historical forces have shaped the religious consciousness of Irish Catholics. Over the centuries Christian and pagan rituals formed a vibrant pre-modern expression of religious belief, while the Great Hunger of the 1840s and the forces that it unleashed gave a particular flavour to Irish Catholicism. Only since the 1960s has this pre-modern mix of faith and culture hit the rocks of modernity. Naturally this has given rise to a certain shapelessness as the icons of an earlier time came under sustained critique. Different groups and individuals will respond in varied ways to this critique, but as we move beyond the iconophilia of an earlier time and the reductionistic certainties of modernity, a new post-modern era of uncertainty and otherness lies ahead of us. In determining new shapes for the Irish Catholicism of the future we will inevitably have to face the reality of the past.

NOTES

1. S. Heaney, *Station Island*, London, Faber & Faber, 1984.
2. B. Friel, *Dancing at Lughnasa*, London, Faber & Faber, 1990.
3. E. Duffy, *The Stripping of the Altars: Traditional Religion in England c.1400-c.1500*, New Haven, Yale University Press, p.8.

4. Quoted in M. McNeill, *The Festival of Lughnasa,* Dublin, Comhairle Bhéaloideas Eireann, 1982, p.126.

5. The issues raised in this controversy have been analysed by Desmond Bowen in *Souperism: Myth or Reality – A Study of Catholics and Protestants During the Great Famine,* Cork, Mercier Press, 1970, and in *The Protestant Crusade in Ireland 1800-70,* Dublin, Gill & Macmillan, 1978.

6. Bowen, *Souperism,* op. cit., p.127.

7. Bowen, op. cit., p.143. Kirby was Cullen's successor as Rector of the Irish College in Rome.

8. D. A. Kerr, *A Nation of Beggars? Priests, People and Politics in Famine Ireland 1846-1852,* Oxford, Clarendon Press, 1994, p. 324.

9. E. Larkin, 'The Devotional Revolution in Ireland', *American Historical Review,* 1972, vol.87, pp. 625-652. Also published in E. Larkin, *The Historical Dimensions of Irish Catholicism,* Washington DC, Catholic University of America Press, 1984, pp. 57-89.

10. M. Baily, 'The Parish Mission Apostolate of the Redemptorists in Ireland, 1851-1898', in R. Gallagher and B. McConvery (eds.), *History and Conscience: Studies in Honour of Sean Ó Ríordán CSsR,* Dublin, Gill & Macmillan, 1989, p. 275.

11. Larkin, *The Historical Dimensions of Irish Catholicism,* op. cit., pp. 77-78.

12. Larkin, op. cit., p. 78.

13. Larkin, op. cit., p. 58.

14. See, for example, T .G .McGrath, 'The Tridentine Evolution of Modern Irish Catholicism, 1563-1962; A Re-examination of the 'Devotional Revolution' Thesis', in R.Ó Muirí (ed.), *Irish Church History Today,* Cumann Seanchais Ard Mhaca, 10 March 1990, pp. 84-99 and Kerr, op. cit., pp. 318-323.

15. McGrath, op. cit., p. 98.

16. Kerr, op. cit., pp. 318-319.

17. Patrick Kavanagh's poem 'The Great Hunger' is still probably the most famous poetic contribution; more recently see Desmond Egan, *In the Holocaust of Autumn,* Newbridge, Co Kildare, The Goldsmith Press, 1994.

18. Tom Murphy's *Famine* was first performed in the Peacock Theatre, Dublin in 1968. His own comments on the drama are notable, see T. Murphy, *Plays: One,* London, Methuen Drama, 1993, pp. ix-xvii.

19. These and other examples can be found in the pages of the *Irish Ecclesiastical Record,* a review which gives an interesting insight into clerical preoccupations since the Famine.

20. This call is well expressed by Dermot Lane, 'Faith and Culture: The Challenge of Inculturation', in D. Lane (ed.) *Religion and Culture in Dialogue,* Dublin, Columba Press, 1993, pp. 11-39.

RELIGIOUS CHANGE IN IRELAND 1981-1990

Christopher T. Whelan and Tony Fahey

The purpose of this paper is to present evidence from the European Values Surveys of 1981 and 1990 on religious values and behaviour in Ireland and to offer some comments on the overall significance of what this evidence has to tell us. The period covered by the surveys in question does not include the revelations of clerical misbehaviour which have rocked the Catholic Church in Ireland in the last two to three years. However, it does relate to a period in which a deep unease about the future of religion had become quite marked in religious circles in Ireland. A sharp decline in religious vocations, the increasingly liberal and secular cast of many developments in public policy, the virtual abandonment by many Catholics of tenets of their religion having to do with reproductive and sexual morality, and a more questioning attitude towards Church authority were among the causes of that unease.

The survey evidence presented here gives us some indication of the pace and extent of change in religious adherence in Ireland. It also enables us to identify the sub-groups in the population where change has been most marked. This gives some hint of the impact of forces such as education, unemployment, urbanisation and gender on religiosity in Ireland. This in turn allows us to consider how far broader social trends such as modernisation may be able to account for religious change in this country.

Church attendance
John Whyte has noted that 'Ireland is unusual in having a large majority not just of Catholics, but of committed and practising

Catholics'.[1] Figure 1 indicates this to be the case with evidence from the European Values Study on the level of church attendance in Ireland in 1981 and 1990 and in Europe.[2]

In Ireland, church attendance remains exceptionally high (over 80 per cent compared to a European average of 30 per cent) and shows only a small decline between 1981 and 1990 (83 to 81 per cent). A sharper decline of about one-fifth was observed in Ireland in attendance more than weekly.

Figure 1

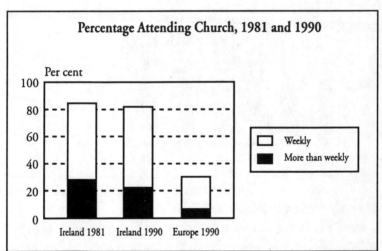

While the differences in attendance in Ireland between 1981 and 1990 are relatively modest the possibility exists that the overall figures may conceal more substantial variations among particular groups. In order to explore this possibility we look at the effects of age, gender, urban-rural location, unemployment and social class.

In Figure 2 we see that church attendance declines by age particularly among the urban group, to 56 per cent of those in their late twenties and early thirties, compared to 90 per cent of those over sixty. The corresponding figures for rural areas are 82 per cent and 93 per cent. The figures for attendance are very similar to those reported by Mac Gréil (1991) on the basis of his survey of religious practice and attitudes among a representative sample of the adult population in 1988/89.

Figure 2

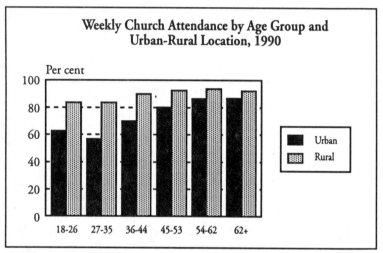

The overall decline is attributable not to an inevitable process of secularisation, affecting individuals in all generations, but to a decline in attachment on the part of the youngest adult groups, which they carry forward with them to some extent as they grow older. Whatever may have caused this, the net effect is that young people have been less and less successfully socialised into institutional religion as Ireland has moved from a position of 'moral monopoly'[3] to *de facto* pluralism, where there is ready access to multiple media sources, values, and life-styles. The data suggests that a significant cultural shift[4] occurred for those who were under the age of thirty-five in 1990, that is, among those born since the mid-1950s. These groups will have grown up since the modernisation and industrialisation policies were initiated in Ireland. Thus, while there is no evidence to support claims for secularisation as far as changes throughout the 1980s are concerned, there are indications that a major cultural shift may have occurred for those born in recent decades. In particular, the trend for the youngest group in 1981 is one that gives some cause for concern for the Catholic Church, since it is by no means certain that the shift towards increased attendance over the life-cycle observed among the earlier groups will hold for this.

The second factor that may affect church attendance is gender, but its effect is likely to be mediated through such factors as urban-rural location (see the breakdown in Figure 3). It is primarily in the urban areas that men have a lesser tendency to attend church with the figure falling to 65 per cent, in comparison with 87 per cent for men in rural areas.

Figure 3

Weekly Church Attendance by Sex and Urban-Rural Location, 1990

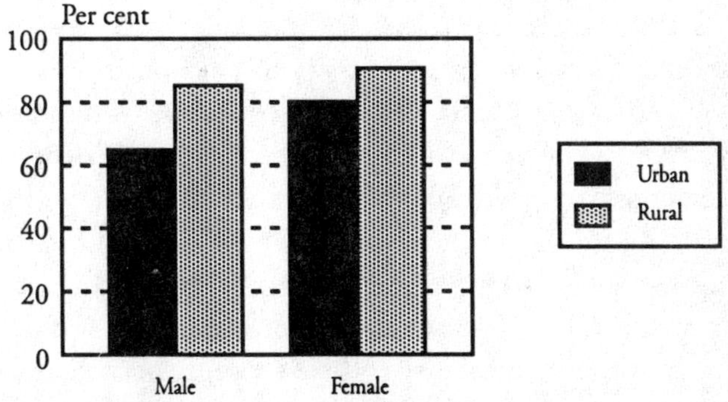

Location also plays a significant role in mediating the impact of unemployment. In rural areas, where there is more likely to be stronger community support as well as strong expectations of church attendance than in urban areas, 75 per cent of the unemployed practise regularly, compared with 90 per cent of those who are not unemployed. In urban areas, however, where social integration is likely to be weaker, unemployment almost halves weekly church attendance, from 75 per cent of those who are not unemployed to only 40 per cent of the unemployed.

Figure 4

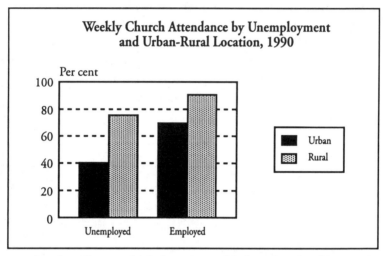

Another factor which interacts with location in this way is what we refer to as basic life-style deprivation. This measure derives from the analysis of dimensions of life-style deprivation carried out as part of the Economic and Social Research Institute poverty project.[5] In the course of this project a set of basic items relating to food, clothing and heating, the enforced absence of which constituted an important component of what was defined as poverty, was identified. The enforced absence of such items has been shown to be strongly related to psychological distress.[6] A comparable set of items was included in the 1990 European Values Study. In fact, there is no difference in the frequency of church attendance in rural areas between those experiencing such deprivation and other people. In urban areas, on the other hand, church attendance is substantially reduced by such deprivation, with a difference of fifteen percentage points emerging in relation to weekly or more frequent attendance.

Apart from the provision of financial rewards, employment provides access to a variety of important categories of experience which are crucial for maintaining self-esteem and facilitating a wide range of social activities. The results of the ESRI Poverty Survey show that the unemployed are substantially more likely to think of themselves as worthless and less likely to feel that they are playing a useful part in things.[7] In view of such findings, it is hardly surprising that the unemployed are less likely to participate in community rituals such as church attendance. It might also be noted that such findings lend no support to the compensatory view of religion.[8]

Exclusion from ordinary living patterns, customs and activities is a standard way of defining poverty. The life-style measure of deprivation provides an indicator of such exclusion, and consequently we would expect it to be related to lower levels of participation in community rituals. In fact, as we have noted, this holds only for those in urban areas. Furthermore, no effect is observed among the unskilled manual class, where such deprivation is not unusual. The impact is concentrated among the other classes, where it is less usual.

These results suggest the possibility that unemployment and deprivation affect church attendance through the impact they have on an individual's self-esteem rather than through the estrangement of significant segments of the working class from Catholicism *per se*. The evidence deriving from the analysis of religious and moral values tends to support this conclusion. It also seems likely that the stronger impact of unemployment in urban areas is due to a combination of (a) the fact that unemployment is more likely to lead to deprivation in urban areas and (b) the fact that the consequences of deprivation for church attendance are stronger in urban than in rural areas.

In the 1990 European Values Study, six social classes were

distinguished, with married women being allocated to the class of their husbands, in the absence of information which would allow us to implement alternative satisfactory procedures.[9] The data shows remarkably little variation in weekly church attendance by social class. Average attendance ranged from 77 per cent for those in the higher professional and managerial occupations to 84 per cent in unskilled manual occupations. The weakness of the social class effect is also contributed to by the fact that primary life-style deprivation makes its strongest impact outside the unskilled manual class. Thus, while the enforced absence of one or more primary life-style items has no effect on weekly church attendance for the unskilled manual class, for all other classes it reduces attendance from 82 per cent where there is no deprivation to 69 per cent where there is.[10]

Figure 5

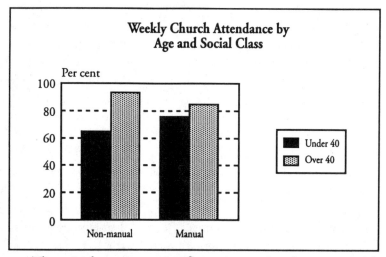

There is, however, a significant interaction between social class and age in their effect on church attendance, as shown in Figure 5. For those aged forty or over, the non-manual respondents are more likely to attend church, with 94 per cent attending weekly or more often, compared with 84 per cent of the manual group. For those under forty, on the other hand, the pattern is reversed, with 78 per cent of the manual class attending weekly or more often, compared with 64 per cent of the non-manual category. Thus, differences in church attendance by age are largely concentrated among non-manual respondents.

Not surprisingly, a similar type of interaction is observed between age and highest level of education. While on average only two-thirds of those with third-level education attended weekly, compared with over four-fifths of those with lower levels of education, the effect is almost entirely to be found among those born since the early 1950s. Once again, it is apparent that significant cultural shifts can be dated from around the 1960s.

Multivariate analysis shows age, third-level education, gender, unemployment, primary life-style deprivation and being in full-time unpaid home duties to have independent effects on frequency of church attendance. If we focus on the extremes, as shown in Table 1, the following comparisons illustrate the cumulative impact of these variables. A sixty-five-year-old woman in full-time unpaid home duties has a 0.98 per cent probability of attending church weekly or more often, while for a twenty-year-old urban unemployed male the probability falls to 0.32 per cent.

Table 1

Cumulative Impact of Socio-Demographic Influences on Church Attendance

	% Attending
65-year-old woman in full-time unpaid home duties	*98*
20-year-old urban unemployed man	*32*

Religious and moral values

Table 2 shows the distribution of responses by age to a number of questions dealing with traditional religious beliefs. Ninety-six per cent of respondents said they believed in God and although this declined slightly across age group, there was no evidence of change over the 1980s. Almost four out of five continued to believe in life after death and slightly higher proportions confirmed their belief in a soul and heaven. Variation across age groups was slightly higher for these items but the percentage in the youngest age groups adhering to these beliefs remained in the high seventies; in each case belief increased slightly across the 1980s. The figures relating to belief in hell are not dissimilar, but belief in hell and the devil are substantially lower, with just about half the respondents responding positively. Trends over time are, once again, weak but the modest decline in such beliefs, taken together with the earlier evidence, provides support for the hypothesis of a move towards a more optimistic interpretation of religion. With the exception of God and sin, variations are quite pronounced on all the items. On average, over 70 per cent of the youngest group believe in life after death, a soul, and heaven, compared with in excess of 90 per cent of the oldest group.

Table 2

Tradition Religious Beliefs by Age Group

	God	Life After Death	A Soul	Heaven	Hell	The Devil	Sin
18-26	92	69	75	78	39	41	79
27-35	96	76	79	82	40	43	84
36-44	93	68	81	80	48	49	83
45-53	97	84	90	87	53	58	88
54-62	97	88	91	92	60	63	87
62+	100	85	94	95	62	64	87
Total	96	78	85	85	50	53	84

Similarly, while over 60 per cent of the latter believe in hell and the devil, this falls to 40 per cent among the younger age groups. An examination of the pattern of results by group gives no indication that these views alter simply as a consequence of age.

Table 3 shows that there has been a significant shift in views regarding the nature of God. Between 1981 and 1990 the proportion believing in a personal God fell from 77 to 67 per cent, while there was a corresponding increase from 15 to 24 per cent in the number whose notion of God was closest to 'some sort of spirit or life force'. Not surprisingly, older respondents are more likely to have an idea of God that conforms to that of a personal God, with eight out of ten holding such a view, compared with fewer than six in ten of those in the youngest age group. However, what is strik-

Table 3

Views on God by Age Group by Time of Survey

	There is a Personal God		There is Some Sort of Spirit or Life Force	
	1981	*1990*	*1981*	*1990*
18-26	65	56	22	32
27-35	68	64	20	28
36-44	81	60	16	32
45-53	85	67	10	22
54-62	83	77	10	18
63+	90	83	7	12
Total	77	67	15	24

ing is that the shift in opinion has occurred in all age groups; in fact, for those aged thirty-five or over, the percentage choosing the 'spirit or life force' option doubles in the period between the two surveys. Thus the evidence suggests that the shift in views is quite general. Finally, the proportion thinking of themselves as religious people actually increased between 1981 and 1990, from 67 to 72 per cent. The figures range from 63 per cent of those aged twenty-five or less to 85 per cent of those aged seventy or over.

Confidence in the Church

Figure 6 documents the extent to which Catholics feel that the Church gives adequate answers to problems. Catholics are much less distinctive in relation to such confidence in the Church than in their religious behaviour or beliefs. Forty-two per cent of Catholics in Ireland have confidence in the Church's ability to meet the moral problems of the individual. Only for the Netherlands, where the figure falls to 29 per cent, can a substantially lower figure be observed. A similar situation pertains in relation to problems of family life, where only 35 per cent express such confidence. Here the highest levels of confidence are expressed in Northern Ireland, Portugal, and Great Britain. These countries also lead the way when the issue is the social problems facing the countries. The figure for Ireland, on the other hand, is not significantly higher, at 34 per cent, than for any of the other countries. Only in relation to the spiritual needs of the individual does Ireland achieve a relatively high score, reaching 71 per cent.

Figure 6

Percentage of Catholics who Consider that the Church gives Adequate Answers to Problems

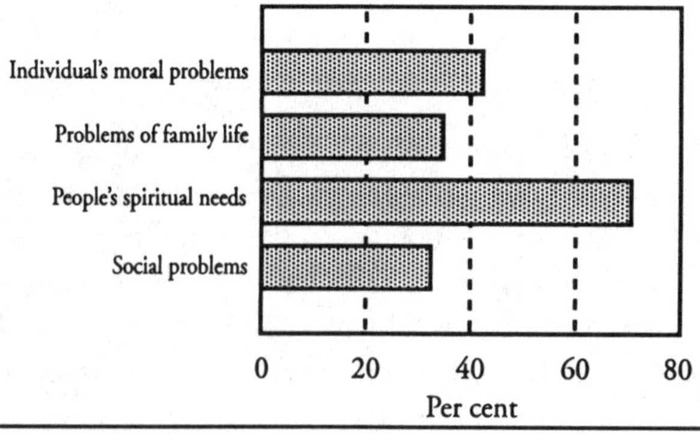

There was little change between 1981 and 1990 in the extent to which Catholics felt that the Church was giving adequate answers to people's spiritual needs. In fact, the relevant proportion rose from 66 to 71 per cent. In relation to family life, however, there was a decline from 48 to 35 per cent, and with regard to the moral problems and needs of the individual the drop was from 53 to 42 per cent. These figures seem to support the view that there has been a general collapse in the 'moral monopoly' of the Church, or, at a minimum, a loss of at least some moral authority.

Implications

By the standards of other western countries, it is clear from this evidence that religious adherence in Ireland is still exceptionally high. It may seem, therefore, that as far as popular allegiance is concerned, talk of a crisis in religion in Ireland is misplaced. There are some important signs of erosion. The post-1950s generations have noticeably lower allegiance, and the fall-off is especially marked at the two ends of the social spectrum – among the poor and unemployed on the one hand, especially in urban areas, and among the university educated on the other. Yet even here, the extent of crisis is relative. Those with the weakest Church affiliation in Ireland – young, unemployed urban males – have slightly higher church attendance rates than the average of all social groups in the rest of Europe.

It could well be argued, therefore, that the thing to be explained about religious affiliation in Ireland is not that it is falling off but that it remains so high. The obvious proximate explanation lies in the strength of religious adherence before the decline set in – the initial position from which the decline began was so elevated that it could sustain much weakening without being seriously undermined. That then throws us back on the further question: How did religious adherence in Ireland become so high in the decades before the 1960s? In the long span of

Christian history, there is nothing normal about the near-universal, highly regular and fully orthodox expression of Catholic affiliation such as was found in Ireland around the middle of the present century. That degree of dutiful fidelity to the Church and its teaching was the product of a period of Catholic expansion which occurred in Ireland from the mid-nineteenth century onwards. The Irish experience was unusual in carrying that expansion to such extremes, but there were numerous other countries where rapid growth occurred not only in the Catholic Church but also in other Christian denominations over the same period (America is the best – but not the only – example, both for Catholicism and for other Christian Churches). Convincing general explanations for that growth are hard to come by. As in Ireland, explanation tends to rely on *ad hoc* factors peculiar to each country rather than on general patterns which apply across national boundaries.

If religious expansion is difficult to explain, so too is contraction, or absence of growth in the first place. Many of the more irreligious parts of Europe today seem always to have been irreligious – some historians suggest that antagonism or indifference to organised religion is of long standing in many European regions, in some cases perhaps going back as far as the medieval era. In those areas, in other words, irreligion should not be mistaken for something new or requiring explanation by reference to modern influences.[11] In other areas, however, definite declines in allegiance to churchly religion have occurred in modern times, though the dates of initiation in these declines vary widely. So, too, do the end-states in which the declines arrive at. In Sweden, for example, formal Church affiliation is very high (at about 90 per cent of the population), but only 10-20 per cent practise their religion with any regularity. In the Netherlands, by comparison, only about half the population claim affiliation to any Church but, about half of these, or a quarter of the total, have strong and sustained attachment.

These observations remind us that there are few general patterns which can serve as guides to what is likely to happen to religious affiliation in Ireland, or as explanatory backdrops to what has happened up to now. We too easily assume that modernity is antagonistic to religion, and that Ireland's high level of religiosity up to now is a mark of its lack of modernity. This assumption in turn leads us to conclude that as Ireland becomes more modern it will inevitably become more irreligious. While there may be some truth in this, when we look in detail at the record of religious adherence in western countries in modern times, we find that there are too many exceptions, anomalies and counter-tendencies for these assumptions to be accepted as general rules.

Modernity *per se* is as capable of strengthening religion as it is of weakening it – witness the example of America over the last hundred years, which was simultaneously the most 'modern' and the most religious of the major regions of the western world. Witness also the strength of Christian fundamentalism in America in the last two decades.

Undoubtedly, certain modalities of modernity, in certain circumstances, can be detrimental to religion, though how and why is not easy to say. From the evidence presented here, for example, it appears that third-level education is associated with lower levels of religious adherence among the post-1950s generation in Ireland but not among older generations of university graduates. Thus it is not so much the increasing incidence of third-level education as its changing cultural content which affects religion in Ireland. We can say something similar about poverty and unemployment. These now reduce religious affiliation, but they do not appear to have done so in the past (recall the intense levels of Catholic devotion which were recorded in the slums of Dublin in the 1930s). Even today, the impact of poverty and unemployment is by no means uniform – it appears to be more profound in urban than in rural areas.

Things like higher education, poverty and unemployment

may therefore be associated with religious decline in Ireland. However, it would be misleading to say that they *explain* religious decline, since they so obviously lacked that impact in the past, not only in Ireland but in many other western countries as well. Rather, there is something about the nature of these things today which gives them a secularising impact that they did not have before.

It is difficult to say what that new element is. It may well have to do with cultural movements rather than changes in the socio-economic structure. Certain cultural developments in recent decades have posed serious challenges to traditional Christian views of the world. Feminism is one of these, and it is worth noting that feminist ideas can have as much an impact on women in farm families in rural Ireland as on professional career women in the major urban industrial centres. These ideas, in other words, do not confine their impact to well-defined socio-economic groups but are diffused in complex ways throughout the social system. The collapse in female religious vocations in recent decades, not only in Ireland but in many parts of the Catholic world, has been far more extreme than the corresponding decline among male vocations and may be one indication of how new thinking about women's roles has helped create a uniform outcome in religious behaviour across quite diverse societies in the west.

One might also refer to the lack of credibility which now attaches to the traditional Christian view of the spirit/body split. Much Christian theology and moral teaching centred on a view of the body as the enemy of spiritual purity and therefore enjoined believers to treat the body and its appetites as a cage from which they had to break free. Today's more holistic view of the human personality would be more likely to interpret an internal war between body and spirit as pathological rather than holy. This is especially so in regard to sexuality, which is now widely seen as something to be cultivated, understood and freely expressed in any of a multiplicity of forms rather than as the chief threat to saintliness.

For those who are concerned about religious decline in Ireland, the very uncertainty about the causes and direction of religious change might well be taken as a hopeful sign. It means that the falling away from religion which has proceeded a certain distance in Ireland has no well-defined inevitability about it. There is no universal force which has always and everywhere undermined religion and which now, at last, has reached Ireland's shores. Rather, there is a far more complex ebb and flow in religious affairs which means that the way is always open for religion to revive as well as decline. Thus, in turn, in the face of secularising tendencies, when religion is ebbing from people's lives, those with religious commitment always have the possibility and the challenge of finding the key that will unlock the door to a new religious flow in Irish life.

NOTES

1. J. Whyte, *Church and State in Modern Ireland, 1923-1979,* 2nd ed., Dublin, Gill & Macmillan, 1980.
2. The countries included in the data for Europe are France, Great Britain, West Germany, Italy, Spain, Portugal, The Netherlands, Belgium and Northern Ireland. Results for Europe are weighted to allow for variation in adult population size.
3. T. Inglis, *Moral Monopoly: the Catholic Church in Modern Irish Society,* Dublin, Gill & Macmillan, 1987.
4. R. Inglehart, *Culture Shift in Advanced Industrial Society,* Princeton, Princeton University Press, 1990.
5. C. T. Whelan, D. Hannan, S. Creighton, *Unemployment, Poverty and Psychological Distress,* Dublin, ESRI, 1991; T. Callan, B. Nolan, C. Whelan, 'Resources, deprivation and the measurement of poverty', in *Journal of Social Policy,* vol. 22(2), 1993, pp. 141-72.

6. Whelan *et al.,* op. cit.
7. Whelan *et al.,* op. cit.
8. R. Stark, W. Bainbridge, *The Future of Religion,* London, University of California Press, 1985.
9. R. Breen, C. Whelan, *Social Class and Social Mobility in Ireland,* Dublin, Gill & Macmillan, 1996.
10. Whelan *et al.,* op. cit.
11. H. McLeod, *Religion and the People of Western Europe 1789-1970,* Oxford, Oxford University Press, 1981.

SELECT BIBLIOGRAPHY

Breen, R. and C. Whelan, *Social Class and Social Mobility in Ireland,* Dublin, Gill & Macmillan, 1996.

Callan, T., B. Nolan and C. Whelan, 'Resources, deprivation and the measurement of poverty', *Journal of Social Policy,* vol 22 (2), 1993, 141-72.

Inglehart, R. *Culture Shift in Advanced Industrial Society,* Princeton, Princeton University Press, 1990.

Inglis, T. *Moral Monopoly: the Catholic Church in Modern Irish Society,* Dublin, Gill & Macmillan, 1987.

Mac Gréil, M., *Religious Practices and Attitudes in Ireland,* Maynooth, Survey and Research Unit, Department of Social Studies, St Patrick's College, 1991.

McLeod, H. *Religion and the People of Western Europe, 1789-1970.* Oxford, Oxford University Press, 1981.

Stark, R. and W. Bainbridge, *The Future of Religion,* Berkeley, University of California Press, 1985.

Whelan, C., D. Hannan, S. Creighton, *Unemployment, Poverty and Psychological Distress,* Dublin, Economic and Social Research Institute, 1991.

Whyte, J. *Church and State in Modern Ireland, 1923-1979,* 2nd ed., Dublin, Gill & Macmillan, 1980.

RELIGION AND MODERNITY:
READING THE SIGNS

Joseph Dunne

The question of method

The growth in ambition and prestige of the social sciences since they first separated out from philosophy (hardly more than a century ago) has threatened to eclipse the parent discipline. A philosopher, then, must welcome the kind of opportunity to test the mettle of the new science that comes with an invitation to respond to Dr Whelan and Dr Fahey's paper.* The most obvious point of interrogation concerns methodology, with attention less on particular findings than on the whole standpoint from which data are analysed and results are presented as authoritative. The rigour on which this claim to authority rests is mainly quantitative: it resides in the exactness with which data are measured and the corresponding detachment and 'objectivity' with which hypotheses are constructed and conclusions drawn. Is this rigour of method paid for, however, by impoverishment of substance? Is there much of significance, in other words, that may be, in principle, unavailable to such a heavily quantitative approach, so that understanding of any domain of social reality must be distorted by exclusive reliance on it? Can this approach ever do justice to the *specificity* of what it seeks to investigate – in this case, the domain of religious belief and practice – or will this specificity always be a casualty of the method which is brought to bear indifferently on every object of its inquiry? Must it not treat religion, indeed, just like every other phenomenon, putting the

* I am indebted to Tony Fahey for helpful background on his and Chris Whelan's paper. I am also grateful to Fergal O'Connor OP and Frank Litton for illuminating converations in the course of writing this paper and to participants at the symposium, especially John Devitt, for thought-provoking responses to the oral presentation of an earlier version of it.

Church on all fours with other institutions such as sporting organisations, political parties or multinational companies? The direction and scope of questioning, then, will be along the following lines: Is its membership holding up, is it filling its stadia, is its product in demand, are its customers satisfied? How is it faring with respect to competitive edge and market share? Is it maintaining a distinctive brand image, while adapting effectively to changing expectations and tastes? Is there confidence in its top management and how is the morale of its employees? Is it expanding or contracting? Is it running a successful operation – where success or failure is defined along roughly standard lines in each case?

Such are the questions that can be pursued through the kind of approach adopted in the European Values Studies on which Whelan and Fahey's analysis is based. Clearly, the questions asked of the respondents are formulated in terms of a small number of precoded categories, so that a great deal of nuance or differentiating detail is forfeit *ab initio*. Within the constraints of these categories respondents are invited to report their perceptions, with no scope, however, for reflection – let alone for any dialogical exchange between respondent and questioner which might evoke a reflective attitude. What will seem especially dubious here to a philosopher is the systematic way in which the question of truth is bracketed. Researchers can hardly avoid some commitment to ensure that respondents truly hold the perceptions which they report – though, as I have intimated, the drastic semantic restrictiveness implicit in their procedures makes the fulfilment of even this commitment deeply problematic. But the more important question of truth never even arises: are *these perceptions themselves* (if we assume that they have been accurately elicited and are actually held by respondents) true? The fact is that this kind of social science forbids itself in principle from asking about the truth of the beliefs (or the good of the practices) which it purports to investigate. Indeed it must be asked whether

even the *meaning* of these beliefs and practices can be appre-
hended through an approach which so insistently maintains the
posture of the third-person observer, renouncing any attempt to
get inside the first-person perspective of participants – all the better to make every such perspective (be it one in business, leisure,
politics, religion or irreligion) equally amenable to its reductionist designs.

A sense of philosophical duty, so to speak, impels me to
advert to these issues on an occasion such as this; but in fact they
are not the issues that I wish to press. This is partly because they
are not perhaps the most constructive ones to pursue here (I sympathise with the animus in Freud's remark, 'methodologists
remind me of people who clean their glasses so thoroughly that
they never have time to look through them') but also because I
do not anyway believe that the authors of the paper I am asked
to respond to are the most appropriate targets for this kind of critique. For they did not, after all, design the framework of the
European Values Studies nor do they show any inclination
towards the kind of doctrinaire positivism which makes the
quantitative, empirical approach so damaging – precisely by
absolutising it and thereby delegitimising any other sources of
knowledge or understanding. To the contrary, it is clear from
Whelan and Fahey's paper (and in particular from the final section on 'Implications') that they see the data collected in the
Survey as being in need of interpretation and recognise that such
interpretation, while it is of course constrained by the data (inso-
far as it is of them that it seeks to give a cogent account), must
still go beyond them for its sources if it is to have anything adequate let alone interesting or rich to offer. Moreover, when such
other sources are not disallowed a priori, then it has to be conceded that the kind of empirical approach which informs the
European Values Studies has its own limited validity. For while
the Church is not *only* an institution, it is – besides whatever theological or faith-informed specification may be given of it (e.g.

'Mystical Body' or 'People of God') – *also* an institution. Accordingly, my purpose in this brief response is to sketch a historical and philosophical perspective which may serve to amplify, though not entirely to confirm, Whelan and Fahey's own reading of the significance of the survey data. But first I shall make a few *ad hoc* comments on some individual findings which seem to me especially noteworthy.

Some piecemeal analysis

The fact that in urban areas 'unemployment almost halves weekly church attendance' is perhaps the most striking of all the findings – all the more so in that other data in the survey do not allow it to be interpreted simply in terms of traditional class differences. For among those in unskilled manual occupations church attendance is in fact higher than it is among those in professional or managerial positions; and the very significant effect of unemployment and 'primary life-style deprivation' in reducing church attendance is most evident among those from higher socio-economic classes. That these findings serve to discredit the 'compensation' theory of religion (classically associated with Marx) will not make them any more palatable to those who believe that the Christian gospel is addressed is a special way to those who are socially excluded.

It is disconcerting to find that according to the 1990 survey over 80 per cent report weekly attendance at church while only 67 per cent claim to believe in a personal God; these figures raise rather acutely the question of what those who do *not* believe in a personal God are doing in church. In fact the figures here might make more sense – and ought to be less worrying for Church authorities – if they were reversed. There would then still be a discrepancy between behavioural observance and personal conviction; but it would be a case of people failing to bring their behaviour so to speak to the level of their beliefs – a failure which, in some degree, surely, is simply part of the human condition. What the actual figures indicate, however, is not a falling-off in behaviour but, more deeply, a falling away of belief – with behaviour, by a lag-effect, still matching the former level of belief. This anomaly is in fact very striking when direct comparisons are made between the 1981 and 1990 data. Whereas church attendance falls by only 2 per cent (from 83 per cent to 81 per cent) throughout the 1980s, belief in a personal God among the two middle age-groups (36-44 and 45-53) falls by a full 20 per cent. And, more starkly, among the same two age groups, over the same nine-year period, belief in God as 'some sort of Spirit or Life force' (as distinct from a Person) doubles.

There is not much sign here of a flight from religion into irreligion, if the latter is taken to entail some full-blooded form of atheism. But there certainly seems to be a marked shift in the nature of what counts as 'religion' – a shift away from faith in a historically specific revelation, articulated theologically in doctrines such as the Trinity and the Incarnation, towards a more diffuse form of what might be called 'spirituality'. The latter seems to be a good deal more sanguine and less punitive than traditional Christianity: only around half the respondents, for instance, believe in 'hell' or the 'devil' (and the fact that even among the oldest age-group (62+) the figure is still below two-thirds belies the fire and brimstone version of religion frequently attributed to the older generation). By contrast, it is interesting that 85 per cent of all respondents believe in 'heaven' – though the fact that only 78 per cent believe in 'life after death' suggests an unorthodox elasticity in the concept of 'heaven' which must be inferred here. The more benign aspect of religion relates to respondents' conception of 'God' and more precisely of his response to human actions. It is interesting – and ironically reassuring – however, that it does not seem to imply an especially optimistic conception of these actions themselves. For it is noteworthy that disbelief in 'hell' and 'the devil' does not correlate with disbelief in 'sin' – in which as many as 84 per cent of all respondents still claim to believe. An intriguing feature of the data here, incidentally, is that the highest level of belief in sin is among the 45-53 age group; this surely throws fresh light on the 'mid-life crisis' and must be worth at least a monograph by some intrepid researcher!

The move towards a kind of indeterminate 'spirituality' which I have discerned in the survey data might attract criticism from those who care for historical density and theological defin- ition. Flannery O' Connor, for instance (at a symposium not unlike the present one), resisted an invitation to 'conceive reli- gion broadly as an expression of man's ultimate concern rather than identify it with institutional Judaism or Christianity or with "going to church"', because there is always a danger that when we try to 'enlarge' our ideas 'we will evaporate them instead, and I think nothing in this world lends itself to quick vaporisation so much as religious concern'. Other important data cited by Whelan and Fahey add distinctly to this impression of vaporisa- tion. A relatively high figure of 71 per cent report that the Church is adequate in meeting 'people's spiritual needs'. On the other hand, only 42 per cent of respondents find the Church adequate in responding to 'individuals' moral problems', while its response to 'problems of family life' and 'social problems' is found adequate by only 35 per cent and 34 per cent respectively. Even if it is wrong to *reduce* the spiritual to the domestic, the social or even the moral, such a gap between it and these latter domains is surely troubling. A Christian must wonder about the quality of family or social life if neither is informed by faith or by faith-inspired hope and charity. But, more pointedly, the ques- tion arises as to what vigour, or even what content, is to be found in a 'spirituality' which has cut itself adrift from such large areas of human life. It may indeed be liberating for lay people and per- haps a relief for priests and bishops themselves that the latter (who, one fears, are assumed to constitute 'the Church' in the survey questions) are kept sequestered in their well-defined 'sacred' spaces. But even if this arrangement is comfortable it is unlikely to be lasting. A religion that is no longer rooted in the soil (even if it often be the hard ground) of people's ordinary lives – or, if this be the wrong end of the metaphor, which no longer bears fruit in their lives – has already lost sap.

Towards a more general account

If we turn now to a more overall consideration of the survey data, Whelan and Fahey are surely right to suggest that what is extraordinary in Ireland's case is not so much the drop in religious practice and affiliation in recent years as the extraordinarily high levels which were already established and against which recent figures can be read as a drop. Plausible historical reasons for what seems a remarkably robust religious culture are not hard to come by. There was the potent mix of religion and nationalism – or the stubborn assertion of a religious identity by a people whose political (and economic) aspirations were so severely thwarted. Then there was the denominational character of virtually the entire educational system, achieved by a combination of an exceptionally effective clerical leadership early on and, later, an unusually compliant state authority. Nowhere else in Europe has public education been so conterminous with denominational schooling. And since schooling itself might be said to be the one truly universal church of the modern age it would be surprising if, once established on denominational lines, it did not have the power to reproduce in each generation high levels of religious adherence. Or again there was the existence of a (primarily rural) culture which integrated religious practice quite seamlessly into a whole pattern of life. Going to church responded to many needs: it allowed people not only to worship their God but to share in a myth and a liturgy which gave meaning, cohesion, uplift, and consolation as well as spectacle, aesthetic satisfaction or plain diversion (think of the Latin Mass or the histrionics of a 'mission'). And of course it also afforded an opportunity to affirm

123

and be affirmed in one's communal membership, to acquire local news, exchange gossip, wear one's Sunday best, repair to the companionship of a nearby hostelry. So well woven was religious belief and practice into the overall fabric of people's lives that it was indeed difficult to disentangle what was genuinely religious in it; even if there was much deeply held faith and not a little hope and charity in this practice, many other needs – which might, and indeed eventually did, find other outlets – were surely being fulfilled through it.

The recent decline in religious practice cannot be understood apart from the disintegration of this wider cultural fabric which was still relatively intact in Ireland up to thirty years ago. Perhaps most expressive of this increasing decline and disintegration is the phrase often heard from people for whom church attendance is no longer meaningful: 'It doesn't do anything for me' (or, a more piquant phrase I heard recently from a parent explaining why it is hard to get teenagers to go to Mass: 'The "cringe factor" has set in'). I want to focus on this contemporary 'me' and, in doing so, to open up a historical and philosophical perspective that will enable me to join issue with Fahey and Whelan about the concept of 'modernity' which figures prominently in their discussion of the implications of the survey data. They question any essential link between modernity and secularisation, pointing out that some regions were characterised by low levels of religious adherence even in pre-modern times and, more significantly, that in some modern societies (notably the United States) levels of religious observance are conspicuously high. I sympathise with this aversion on their part to any general thesis about secularisation as an inexorable process and with their properly empirical respect for the many differences which would submerge any such thesis under 'too many exceptions, anomalies and counter-tendencies'. Still, in what follows I shall risk pushing the analysis further and speculate more boldly (and, I admit, with rather less circumscription by the survey data) than they do. It may well be that in doing so I shall not only go beyond what they would consider warranted but also drive in a different (or perhaps simply in a more definite) direction than they would wish to take. My hope of course is that these brief remarks will be found illuminating – so that philosophical and sociological perspectives may here be seen as complementary rather than antagonistic, or simply indifferent, to each other.

Capitalist modernisation and cultural modernism

I would first of all distinguish more explicitly than Whelan and Fahey between *capitalist modernisation* and *cultural modernism.* The former has to do with technological and economic development and therefore with the industrialisation and urbanisation mentioned in their paper; the quite marked differences in the survey between rural and urban respondents indicate that this is significantly correlated with a decline in religious practice in Ireland. Still, the authors are correct, I believe, to suggest that modern secularisation 'may well have to do with cultural movements rather than changes in socioeconomic structure'. They do not have much to say about such movements, however, other than to point to third-level education as a significant locus for their diffusion and to specify their content in terms of feminism, as well as changing attitudes to the human body and sexuality. But there is a story that can be told about what I am calling 'cultural modernism', which roots it in the eighteenth century Enlightenment and sees it, in intention and effect, as both more universalist and more secularising than Whelan and Fahey's paper suggests. This story is a complex one. (Quite apart from the recent invasion of the prefix 'post' into the whole discussion, cultural modernism cannot be separated from capitalist modernisation; for the latter has provided the material conditions for the former just as the former has provided some of the ideological formations conducive to the latter). But I shall very briefly identify what I take to be three central, and intertwining, strands in the modernist narrative and then ponder their impact on the fortunes of religion in the modern world.

First, there is the new emphasis on persons as individuals, with an inherent dignity based on their capacity for autonomy and hence with inalienable rights and liberties; this emphasis is seen as the basis of a democratic form of politics and is often articulated in terms of philosophical liberalism, with a high premium on values such as tolerance and pluralism. Second, there is a movement towards the socialised provision for basic needs – especially education, health, welfare and housing – culminating in the post-war Welfare State. Third, there is a valorisation of interiority and subjectivity, concern for a richer and more intense inner life, striving for greater levels of personal authenticity as well as interpersonal intimacy, a whole new fascination with the 'self', fuelling drives towards more self-exploration, self-expression and self-fulfilment. Together, these three strands represent the edifying side of the Enlightenment legacy and, incorporating a fair deal of Romanticism (especially in the third strand), they constitute what might be called the high ground of modernity.

If we ask about the import of modernity in this sense for organised religion, there are two conflicting ways in which the story can be told. On one telling, this whole movement may be seen as having occurred precisely in opposition to religious and ecclesiastical authority. It is a story of struggle, in which organised religion was one of the most important obstacles which had to be overcome. Only in spite of the churches did the whole movement progress; it was essentially a movement of emancipation and foremost among the forces that we needed to be emancipated from were the shackles of religious authority and tradition. Now this is a quite common way of reading the modern narrative. It seems peculiarly plausible in the Irish context and is often indeed an unspoken assumption in hostile media treatment of the Catholic Church in Ireland. And, clearly, it discredits religion, giving us every motivation to leave it behind.

But a quite different, and indeed contrary, interpretation is also possible. One might claim that all three waves I have identified in fact arose from, and were inspired by, Christianity itself. The emphasis on universal rights and the dignity of each person, then, is seen as crystallising out of Christianity as a universalist religion with a concern for the eternal destiny of each individual soul (and it is seen as indicative that democracy and human rights have not arisen historically from the religions of Asia or the Far East). Second, the concern to tend the sick or educate the young or support the poor, as it is gradually incorporated in the agenda of the nation state, is seen as itself the devolution onto political institutions of an ethical imperative, rooted in the gospels, which had always been at the heart of Christian evangelical work. Third, it might be claimed that the whole modern concern with interiority was already prefigured in disciplines and practices of the spiritual life which had been part of the Christian tradition right back to St Augustine and the early Fathers of the Church (so that for instance the confessor or spiritual director is forerunner of the therapist or counsellor).

Now on the second reading secularisation does not betoken the rise of peculiarly anti-religious forces in the modern era. Rather, it is the alienation of the spirit of Christianity itself into domains of legal, educational, political, social and psychological endeavour that then become autonomous – that cut themselves off, erasing the traces of their religious ancestry. If this second interpretation (a Hegelian one) seems more benign to religion, it may be no less damaging to it. For if on the first reading religion is discredited, on this second reading it is made redundant – in fact, it is seen as having, by a peculiar kind of *kenosis,* made itself redundant. Here one may think of orders and congregations of religous sisters and brothers who find themselves in crisis because the work they were established to do or the needs they sought to respond to are now done or met by an array of specialists – teachers, nurses, social workers etc. – in the 'public services sector' or the 'caring professions'. Or the priest finds that queues for the confessional have gone down to a trickle while counselling and psychotherapy multiply and flourish. Nor is it only a case of practising religious finding themselves derelict. There is also the spectacle of many theologians and religious thinkers chasing enthusiastically after every manifestation of the modern (or, increasingly, 'post-modern') spirit, eager to embrace it and to demonstrate to all-comers the unimpeachability of their modernist credentials.

The self and its shadow

I find the second of these two interpretations more interesting as well as more persuasive; but whichever of the two interpretations one adopts one must see the modern story against a further backdrop of radical change which defines modernity, creating a chasm between it and the pre-modern world. In the pre-modern world persons understood themselves within the limits of a cosmic order which was created, transcendently grounded and given. One was located within a natural and supernatural universe that had priority over oneself and provided the point and purpose of one's activities, indeed of one's very existence. For the modern self, by contrast, that framework has all but collapsed. And this collapse is not any longer just at the level of philosophical argument; it is a matter of lived experience – we are all modern selves (more or less) now. There is something radically anthropocentric about our given perspective: hence the apprent finality and indefeasibility of the simple assertion, 'it doesn't do anything for me'. This is a 'me' deeply anchored in its own subjective stance, whence it defines what it will find valuable or real. The self has become the centre of its own experience and must itself discover and certify the meaningfulness of what it experiences. Since there is no longer a pre-existing order within which it finds itself and is defined, any order that can now exist must first pass *its* test of plausibility, credibility and acceptability.

Now it seems to me as a philosopher that the fortunes of religion can be adequately understood only in relation to what tale you tell (or believe or experience) about this self. There is an upbeat, sunny-side-of-the-street tale told by those who retain the passionate optimism of the Enlightenment or who suppose that the vision of the great Romantic writers (poets as well as philosophers) can somehow be translated from radical critique into lifestyle recipes. But there is also a more sombre, downbeat version: that this self may not be up to the task indicated by its own most expansive rhetoric; that the autonomous and authentic self all too easily becomes the acquisitive or narcissistic self; and that a self's scope for exercising autonomy is anyway severely compromised by the growth of an environment that is ever more technically administered and controlled. In this environment public space and communal life contract as genuinely participative practices become harder to sustain and, as a consequence, greater demands are made of privatised experience – especially in the spheres of intimacy and sexuality. Even if this private space appears as a refuge from the increasingly rationalised arenas of the market economy and the state apparatus, it itself may have little resistance to the same technicist imperatives that have more obviously colonised the worlds of work and politics. The private self that has become a connoisseur of its own needs then finds that the fulfilment of these needs lies increasingly in the hands of specialist providers; it has become, in other words, a consumer and a client. It is assailed not only by goods and commodities but by fabricated definitions of merit, performance and satisfaction; and an army not only of advertisers and vendors but of therapists, gurus and consultants ('new age' as well as 'modern') ministers to its self-esteem, inner harmony, assertiveness, personal productivity, etc.

All this of course is for the middle class and the well-employed. Meanwhile, the effects of social and communal disintegration manifest themselves more rawly in the sprawling estates, increasingly ghettoised on the outskirts of our cities, where huge levels of unemployment and poor social and cultural facilities conspire to make family life and the rearing of children a precarious undertaking. Or there are the old people living alone within a stone's throw of our most affluent streets who have been spat out of the remunerative economy when their capacity for productive labour has been exhausted and who strive to maintain dignity often in the face of quiet desperation. Or there are the destitute people, many of them young, who live a twilight existence in hostels or on the streets, often defeated by alcohol or drugs, never having found the combination of means, calculation and luck necessary for finding a niche in 'normal' life. These lives remain as the shadow or suppressed side of the dominant modernist project, being a sign of contradiction to its most inflated discourses of the self.

It seems to me worthwhile to air this darker story about modernity, if only as a salutary counter to the complacency and delusion that accompany any strong telling of the sunny tale which – as the one favoured by those with various kinds of power in our society – may justifiably be called the dominant story. There is a truth, however, which is captured by *neither* story: resistance in the 'life-world' to technicism and narcissism and, despite the pressures, the buoyancy of ordinary decencies in many people's lives. In so far as this resistance no longer simply draws on the residual capital of a traditional culture but becomes more reflective and explicit – as perhaps it inevitably must – it itself bears the marks of modernity. It puts a fair reliance on experience, or rather on a first person perspective which makes it important for people to attend to what their experience actually is before they can listen meaningfully to their own or anyone else's voice telling them what it ought to be. The liberty that appears here allows openness to a fuller range of experience and also extends the range of people whose experiences count – whose stories can be heard – most conspicuously to women and children but also to other more specific and previously silenced groups. This same liberty also calls out for greater critical discernment; for of course it can rightly be said that 'experience' in itself is no assurance against manifold evils and that 'openness' can admit all kinds of horrors. This fact may be sufficiently off-set, however, by the no less deniable fact that closedness and the pre-empting of people's experience by those above them in station was no proof, either, against terrible abuses. In any case, people whose search for goodness or for joy leads them to resist the fabricated versions of contentment pressed upon them in contemporary society are no more hospitable to the enjoinments of any authority that cannot somehow be made persuasive in the crucible of their own experience. Such people are not thereby left as solitary selves. For they are scarcely conceivable outside webs of relationship in which their characters and judgements are both challenged and confirmed. They are creatures, in other words, of community – the value of which we are forced to recognise even as its reality can no longer be relied on as given.

Conclusion

What, then, might be the fate of religious belief in the working out of this whole drama of modernity – right through to its most extreme consequences which are now fashionably labelled as 'postmodernist' and either castigated as symptoms of irrationality and disintegration or celebrated as signs of 'decentering' and 'difference'? It would, I think, be an act of *hubris* to attempt an answer to this question in the final section of a short paper – or perhaps in any piece of writing. It may always be said of course that the task of realising and understanding the gospel in relation to alien culture is what it has ever been: the whole history of theology, as of the Church itself, has been one of ongoing confrontation, assimilation and development. This reminder of continuity in constant discontinuity and sometimes across radical rupture only offers perspective, however; it does not reassure us that there is not after all something truly unprecedented in the challenge which the Church faces in the modern world, much less instruct us as to how this challenge is to be met. I have said

enough, I hope, to show that the confident sense of having overcome religion and consigned it to the graveyard of history (and
replaced it with a bright new humanism secreting truth, justice,
happiness and peace), which fired the eighteenth-century
Enlightenment as well as the nineteenth-century belief in
Progress, rings hollow at the end of our battered century – as
some of its most reflective writers now amply attest. But believers would have learned little if they were to suppose that they can
now dance on the grave of modernity or that in its dark spaces a
religious light must surely shine. A proper historical sense ought
rather to inform us that modernity is a quite recent experiment
whose issue is still uncertain (we might learn from Mao Tse-
Tung's alleged answer to the question, 'What were the most
important consequences of the French Revolution?' – 'It's too
early to say'). Moreover, we are all (at least in this part of the
world) caught up in this experiment, with no easy way out and
no way at all back.

'Experiment' is a misleading term here if it suggests a single
clear-cut idea or action-path being put to the test and unequivocally confirmed or refuted. Far too many disparate and often
conflicting things are conflated if we suppose that there is one
internally consistent referent of the word 'modernity' – as we easily
do if we focus too exclusively on what I have identified above as
its debit-side or, more particularly, assume that modernity is itself
without resource in recognising this debit and subjecting it to the
most penetrating critique. Christians make a bad mistake, I
believe, if they fail to recognise the moral and spiritual sources
generated in and through 'the making of the modern identity' –
just as they do also (to reinforce an earlier point) if they miss the
contribution of Christianity itself, in various strands, to the making of this same identity. The mistake here, in other words, is to
polarise Christianity and modernity and to suppose that it must
be a choice of one or the other – a mistake that is compounded
when this choice is presented as one between a spiritual religion

on one side and, on the other, crass materialism, shallowness and a moral void. It is a matter, rather, of being a Christian *and* a modern, i.e. a modern Christian, which is perhaps the only kind now that one can be – or (if one is serious about history and community, and therefore about evangelisation) ought to want to be. Just how this is to be lived and understood remains of course extraordinarily vexing.

What is gone forever, we must assume (even if in Ireland it is only very recently gone), is a situation of the kind that lasted in Christian Europe for a millennium, one in which belief was not only uncontested but – such was the depth of its seepage through the total culture – incontestable. Gone, too, is the related phenomenon of a faith anchored in cosmic reference-points and relying on an entirely public and uniformly shared register for its expression. It is well to recognise, though, that this fate which has befallen Christianity is now the fate of all beliefs or visions that lay claim to people's minds and hearts: they coexist (or perish) with a multiplicity of rival claims in a milieu of (at least implicit) debate and contestation; and each of them comes to be held not simply as a set of doctrines but rather as personally indexed, or as refracted through a particular sensibility. The language I use here (of 'indexing' and 'refraction') is borrowed from Charles Taylor's magisterial *Sources of the Self,* which brings a unique breadth of sympathy to its attempt to understand and do justice to the modern identity, while being entirely free from the coldness to religion which marks the work of so many modern interpreters and critics. Taylor is fully alive to the strongly reductionist tendencies in central streams of modern philosophy and, more broadly, to the distorted nature of much of the self-understanding of modernity (indeed few contemporary thinkers have done such yeoman work in combatting just this reduction and distortion). What is particularly valuable in the present context, however, is his tracing of the many paths that modern writers have explored – have been driven to – in their quest for what I called above 'moral and spiritual sources' (another Taylorian locution). It is true that these are paths of *dispossession* and that in all of them, especially those of the great modernists (in the more specialised literary sense – e.g. Joyce, Mann, Eliot, Pound, or Beckett and Celan) the journey is inexorably inward or reflexive. It is not, on that account, however, subjectivist – that is to say, it is not enclosed within the orbit of the self, either celebrating the latter's supposedly sovereign powers or devising any of the countless substitutes, compensations or correctives for its palpable lack of power that litter the contemporary scene. (Among the latter, of course, may well be 'religion' or, rather, the more ersatz versions of it that flourish especially in the United States – a fact, incidentally, which might make one more circumspect than Whelan and Fahey about pointing to this country as the great counter-example to any thesis coupling modernisation and secularisation.)

With reference to the self entrenched theoretically by the founding figures of modern philosophy (perhaps especially Descartes and Hobbes) and still assiduously pursued by the established culture of modernity, this art is ascetical: by a *via negativa* it reduces to poverty of spirit. When it does not end in nihilism, however, it is also often (again in Taylor's term) epiphanic: through it, something otherwise unavailable or inexpressible about the world, or its limits, or our way of being in it, is revealed. And this revelation (which is never just at the artist's disposal and is anyway quite unachievable through theoretical discourse) is also an affirmation. It affirms something about the world (even if it does not represent or describe it) so that those who participate in this affirmation – who come, so to speak, within its field of force – can be transformed by it.

This reference to epiphanic art at the end of the paper is not intended to produce a *deus ex machina*. There are notorious difficulties with any attempt to aestheticise morality or politics, let alone religion; the artist should not be expected to cut a better figure as priest than as moralist or politician. And even if epiphanic art is seen as a kind of training for transcendence it remains that some of its own greatest practitioners would certainly not entertain a *religious* interpretation of this latter term. Besides, all of this must in any case seem far removed from the solid data on bodies in pews that was our point of departure. Despite the apparently reassuring import of these data for Church leaders, however, discernment of spirit in these times (I have wanted to suggest) must lead us to ask whether the realities of grace and sacrament can still be mediated in their old forms. And here perhaps the Church needs to be properly arrested by our thematic phrase, 'it doesn't do anything for me'. For it may not be enough, after all, simply to debunk the pretentions and illusions of the 'me'; perhaps the 'it', too (i.e. the liturgy as presented and indeed the Church's wider mode of embodiment), can no longer speak adequately to those whose spirits have been chastened in the journey through modernity. What new forms, then, might emerge? The real wilderness experience for the contemporary Church lies in the honest acknowledgement that there is no obvious answer to this question. But it is for just this reason that Taylor's notion of the epiphanic (a term which James Joyce of course had already taken over from the Christian lexicon) seems to me to be suggestive. It points to chinks through which what is other than ourselves breaks through with a power to show us as – in part indeed to make us – other than we thought.

It may be of the nature of these chinks that we can never be sure in advance just where to look for them. Still, hope seems best directed now to those prophetic places where the Church finds itself as a broken body among poor and afflicted people. By a fitting irony, it may be in areas of 'primary life-style deprivation' – which on the evidence of the surveys show a marked decline in church attendance – that the most promising signs of new life are to be discerned in the Church. These are signs of small groups of people unusually exposed in their life-experience and correspondingly more radical in their attempts to interpret it. These groups seem post-traditional in that they arise as the traditional parish structure goes into decline; one might say they are engaged in 'the construction of new forms of community' or that they anticipate 'another – doubtless very different – St Benedict'. By the same token, however, it is perhaps through them that the tradition is now most alive. For in searching for exemplars or for a wisdom that addresses their lives they see how diminished we are by an oversaturated present and look keenly to different layers of religious traditions – their own, primarily, but not perhaps exclusively. The difficulties (not least that of maintaining unity in diversity) for a Church carried forward by such groups are surely great – though not too great if they are indeed outstanding signs in the story of God's love for the world.

NOTE

Sources of the Self (Cambridge: Cambridge University Press, 1989) subjects the modern identity to differentiated critique while attempting, through a work of 'retrieval', to save what Taylor sees as its best, though often submerged, aspirations. A more compact and in many ways more accessible statement of the argument of this *magnum opus* is to be found in Taylor's much shorter book, *The Ethics of Authenticity* (Cambridge, MA.: Harvard University Press, 1991). A quite different attempt to defend modernity, through critical 'reconstruction', is to be found in the work of Juergen Habermas, especially in *The Theory of Communicative Action*, vol.1, *Reason and the Rationalisation of Society* and vol. 2, *The Critique of Functionalist Reason* (Boston: Beacon Press, 1984 and 1987), where the distinction I make above between 'capitalist modernisation' and 'cultural modernism' is considerably elaborated; Habermas builds on Max Weber's analysis of modernisation and on the work of the Frankfurt School (of which Theodor Adorno and Max

Horkeimer's *Dialectic of Enlightenment* [London: Verso, 1979] is a classic text). For altogether more trenchant and thoroughgoing opposition to modernist pretentions, or the 'Enlightenment legacy', see the work of Alasdair Mac Intyre, with its strong pre-modern sympathies (especially *After Virtue,* [London: Duckworth, 1981] from the last paragraph of which I take the phrases 'construction of new forms of community' and 'another – doubtless very different – St Benedict') or, in a very different, more ambivalent, and 'post-modernist' mode, the work of Michel Foucault (the many phases of which can be helpfully accessed through Hubert L. Dreyfus and Paul Rabinow, *Michel Foucault: Beyond Structuralism and Hermeneutics,* Chicago: University of Chicago Press, 1983). I attempt a fuller account of central predicaments of modernity and of philosophical resources for an adequate conception of the self in *Back to the Rough Ground: 'Phronesis' and 'Techne' in Modern Philosophy and in Arisotle* (Notre Dame and London: University of Notre Dame Press, 1993) and 'Beyond Sovereignty and Deconstruction: the Storied Self', in R. Kearney, ed., *Hermeneutics of Action: Ricouer at Eighty* (New York: Sage, 1996). For recent theological work that is deeply informed by the very lively philosophical debate about modernity, while affirming a Christian vision, see e.g. John Milbank, *Theology and Social Theory: Beyond Secular Reason* (Cambridge: Basil Blackwell, 1990) and Stanley Hauerwas, *Despatches from the Front: Theological Engagements with the Secular* (Durham and London: Duke University Press, 1994). The quotation from Flannery O'Connor is from 'Novelist and Believer' – a paper delivered to a symposium on Religion and Literature at Sweetbriar College, Virginia, in March 1963 – in *Mystery and Manners* (New York: Farrar, Straus and Giroux, 1969), pp. 154-55.

ASPECTS OF THE SECULARISATION OF IRISH SOCIETY 1958-1996

Marguerite Corish

Introduction

The thinking on secularisation is heir to a major shift which defines modernity. In the wake of the revolutions which took place in England in 1688, in the United States in 1776 and in France in 1789, society is no longer seen as the extension of the divine intention, but rather as the result of human will and actions. This entirely new way of looking at the world has become known as the Enlightenment, that is the emergence of a new kind of historical consciousness: the causal role of God was put into perspective as the stress was laid on the emancipation of human beings. This emancipation, which reduces the role traditionally played by religion in society, both as an institution and as a body of belief, carries with it major consequences for society as a whole. Secularisation can be seen as the process by which the structuring role of religion in society is gradually eroded, as people themselves give shape and meaning to the world around them. It is a process of change from one type of society to another. Western societies have evolved from transcendence to immanence, from a state in which God was the structuring principle to a state in which human beings are responsible for their own destiny. In historical terms, secularisation is an enriching time as it corresponds to a transition period.

Western societies have evolved from a state where the Catholic religion used to be the structuring principle to a state where it became either a minority religion after the Reformation, or an institution amongst others when it remained a majority religion. No such major change could take place without a certain amount of tension and even conflict between the forces of tradition and the forces of modernity. In order to come to terms with the tension and conflict engendered by change, we resort to questioning and debating, and it is in this sense that secularisation is productive.

Secularisation has been considered here in the wider context of western societies; it has, indeed, been typical of the evolution of western capitalist societies and has been seen as a concomitant of industrialisation, urbanisation and general materialism and individualism. However, it must be stressed that the Irish situation has been very different from that of other western societies, mainly because of its colonial status. When other western societies were trying to shake off the yoke of religion, Ireland, on the contrary, was rallying around the Catholic Church as a means of asserting national identity against the foreign oppressor. Emmet Larkin has put forward the thesis that the 'devotional revolution'[1] experienced by Irish people in the last quarter of the nineteenth century replaced in terms of national identity the cultural and linguistic distinctions which had been lost, both as a result of occupation and the Great Famine. Moreover, as it happens, the English belonged to a different Church, which made it even easier for Irish people to identify with the Catholic Church. One consequence of the British occupation was that the forces of clericalism and nationalism became close allies in the latter part of the nineteenth century particularly, and became legitimised after independence. Catholicism and nationalism became the two main pillars on which Irish political culture rested. Because being Irish became synonymous with being Catholic for 95 per cent of the population of the Free State from 1922 onwards, it has proved difficult not to be a Catholic in Ireland, for fear of losing one's national identity.

Because each country has its own history, each country has its own form of secularisation. In France, where the Catholic Church had been closely linked to the state until the Revolution – we had an absolute monarchy of divine right,[2] with the clergy being one of the three political forces in government – historically, secularisation has a clear political content: it meant separation of Church and state, which translated into a secular state apparatus, secular schools, and a network of secular health and welfare services. At the end of the nineteenth century and in the early twentieth century, very bitter conflicts flared up on those issues between 'republican secularists' and clerical parties. In Ireland, there are no Church parties (such as Christian Democrats, for instance, as in Italy and Germany) and no anti-clerical parties either. There was and there is no organised, sustained, long-term campaign for the secularisation of the state, or for the secularisation of schools. The Catholic ethos suffused all areas of society: individuals, institutions and political parties, so there was no need for separate Catholic institutions or political parties. On the one hand, the process of secularisation was and is rather a series of crises that flare up, on Mother and Child Schemes, abortion and divorce referenda, and then peter out, creating very few permanent organisations, parties or associations.[3] On the other, there is no doubt that the whole fabric of Irish society has changed gradually and in some areas dramatically since the end of the 1950s.

What is striking about Ireland is that it changed much later than its western counterparts but, as a result, at a much more rapid pace. When Ireland became industrialised and urbanised, which happened roughly a century later, all the technological, medical and legal knowledge and apparatus already existed and were already in place in other parts of the world, and very close indeed in Britain and other European countries, or in the rest of the English-speaking world. Efficient means of transport and communication, the television, modern means of contraception, were all freely available to the private consumer at that stage and were becoming part of everyday life. So, Ireland could pick and choose as everything was already there, and it could move fast. For instance, in the area of sexual morality, Ireland has moved from banning all artificial contraception to allowing all forms of contraception, including the sale of condoms without any lower age limit; from laws criminalising homosexuality to laws on homosexuality which rank among the most liberal in the world; from a total ban on divorce to the possibility of the introduction of no-fault divorce into Irish law, all in just sixteen years (1979-1995).

However, this process of change has not occurred without hesitations, questions and even tensions; the extremely close result in the 1995 referendum on divorce testifies to the ever present conflict between tradition and modernity. In Ireland, the weight of tradition is strong, for reasons already mentioned. Studying the secularisation of Ireland means constantly bearing in mind the ambiguous relationship that Irish people have with religion and its accompanying set of moral values. This is not to say that this dichotomy does not exist in other societies, or that the need for religion is strong only in Ireland; it is just that, because of Ireland's past, the phenomenon has been accentuated; the difference is one of degree only. The American sociologist Robert Nisbet[4] has in fact come to the conclusion that people were characterised far more by their desire for stability rather than by their desire for change. Indeed, thinkers, commentators and sociologists of religion hold varying views in their evaluations of the phenomenon of secularisation in Irish contemporary society. If voices coming from the media have been quick to herald the demise of religion in Ireland, scholars have been less so. For instance, Michael Hornsby-Smith has argued that 'in spite of considerable social turmoil and the religious transformations over the past three decades, it is clear that modernisation processes have not been accompanied unambiguously by secularisation'.[5] He is echoing Andrew Greeley's analysis which tends to play down the secularisation thesis in view of 'the survival of religion in the midst of the crisis which is alleged to have been destroying it'.[6] In an article entitled 'Ireland: the Exception That

Proves Two Rules' Máire Nic Ghiolla Phádraig wrote: 'The last twenty years have brought about some erosion, but by and large the Republic of Ireland may be characterised as an unself-consciously Catholic state.'[7] However, it must be borne in mind that this was written in 1988 and a lot has happened since, varying from a sharp decrease in Mass attendance and vocations to a spate of revelations of child sexual abuse by priests and extreme neglect of children in orphanages run by nuns, to the latest constitutional change in family law.

Yet there is an overall consensus on the fact that Irish society has undergone major changes since the late 1950s and early 1960s. The traditional image of Ireland has faded. Though signs of faith such as public shrines, regular devotions and reception of the sacraments, the Angelus twice a day on national radio and television, the naming of Aer Lingus planes and Irish Ferries boats after saints, are still numerous, there are also signs which point towards a secularisation of society such as the decline of some traditional religious practices and beliefs, the decrease in vocations, and, consequently, in the numbers of religious staff in schools and health services, which were traditionally Catholic strongholds in Ireland. That a process of social and cultural change in which many, perhaps most, areas of human life – economics, business, politics, law, education, medicine, and so on – have become detached from the influence of religion and have attained their own autonomous existence and value can scarcely be doubted.

When studying secularisation, one point must be made: secularisation does not mean hostility to religious values. In April 1991, in Castlereagh Borough near Belfast, a referendum was held by the Council about the opening of a commercial centre on Sundays. The results showed that 13,000 were in favour and 2,000 against. Alan Carson, DUP mayor of the Borough, faced with strong criticism from his own supporters, answered: 'We do not wish to legislate for other people's consciences' – this might be a good definition of a secular state – but he added that his people were good, religious people.[8] You have the same phenomenon in Israel; lay people might campaign against civil religious legislation, for example banning the sale of pork, but when asked, they all say they do not eat pork themselves. So either they tell the truth, or they do eat pork but cannot say it publicly.

Moreover, secularisation is not a uniquely linear process, ultimately leading to the death of religion and religious values. Rather, it means that religion does not hold the same position in society as it previously did and that, as a result, it has to adapt to its new position. Referring to the etymology of the word proves helpful; the term 'secular' derives its origin from the Latin term *soecularis,* meaning 'profane', which comes from *soeculum,* 'the world'. In the Middle Ages, the phrase 'secular clergy' was used for the first time in 1260 to designate the clergy who lived in parishes, that is in 'the world',[9] as opposed to the 'regular clergy' who belonged to religious orders and who lived apart from 'the world'. Part of the problem when dealing with the notion of secularisation lies with the choice of the historic context against which the 'secular' society is set. When we speak of the secularisation of Ireland from the end of the 1950s, we must bear in mind that, although Irish people's allegiance to Christianity dates back to Saint Patrick's evangelisation and their allegiance to the Catholic Church dates back to the Reformation, the way in which people have practised and lived their faith has changed greatly. For example, Mass attendance, which is often used as a measure of secularisation, has only been extremely high in Ireland for the past 150 years. Prior to this, the Irish Catholic Church lacked seminaries, clergy and churches; Emmet Larkin has estimated that regular Mass attendance would have been possible for at most 42 per cent of Catholics as late as 1840.[10] For the purpose of this particular study, we will set the present Irish context against that of an extremely religious one prior to 1960, and depending on the data considered, we could even say prior to the 1970s. The date 1958 was chosen because at that point, the Irish state, faced with very poor economic achievement and massive emigration, made a clear decision which was to alter radically the type of policies pursued up to then, and which would change the fabric of society itself in many areas. With its Programme for Economic Expansion,[11] the Irish government chose to draw a line on the past and move forward.

The changing societal context: underlying factors and agents
The new economic policy put in place by the government in 1958 was in fact the starting-point of a new era; it then created the right kind of environment for new issues to come to the fore in Irish society. The major transformations which this entailed have now become commonplace: industrialisation, urbanisation, and general rationalisation. At societal level, it translated into consumerism and individualism. People saw their standard of living improve, giving them access to consumer goods, television and foreign influences. New concerns preoccupied Irish people; there was a dissolution of the hegemony of Catholicism and nationalism as people started to focus on new issues such as social justice issues, the environment and women's place in society. In Ireland, secularisation actually means a breakaway from the founding values, both national and religious. Besides, the conflict in Northern Ireland from 1969 and Ireland's joining of the EEC in 1973 have led Irish people to reflect upon the nature of Irish identity in a new light.

Three of the main agents of secularisation in Irish society, urbanisation, feminism, and the media, have irretrievably altered the old moral order. With the advent of urbanisation and feminism, the old community structures and the traditional family, both mainly rural-based, collapsed; the moral order which had prevailed so far, based on the Catholic ethos, was no longer suited to the new urban, individualistic life-style. The media, and especially television, reflected these changes, but also acted as an eye-opener for Irish society.

The government's new economic policy resulted in a significant shift of employment from agriculture to manufacturing and services, which gave rise to a move from rural areas to urban areas where industries and offices were situated. The 1961 Statistical Abstract gives a figure of 413,000 persons at work in agriculture in 1960, whereas the 1994 Statistical Abstract gives a figure of 144,000 in 1993, which gives an idea of the extent to which the agricultural sector has decreased in the period we are studying. The number of people at work in industry (312,000) and services (690,000) in 1993 compared to those at work in agriculture is also a meaningful indicator that Ireland has definitely moved from being a rural society relying almost uniquely on its agriculture.[12]

Dublin in particular was the seat of new developments; its population increased by one-sixth between 1971 and 1978, faster than any western European capital. The result is that around one-third of the total population now lives in the greater Dublin area.[13] Rural communities had already started to break up with massive emigration in the 1950s; rural drift to the cities accentuated the trend. Not only has numerical loss of population, mainly of the young, affected the traditional structure of Irish rural society, but when those who left returned to their communities of origin, on occasional or regular visits, they brought with them from abroad or from Irish cities a different and more liberal value system, less influenced by the Catholic ethos. Besides, Irish people became generally more mobile; either economic necessity dictated that they move to where employment was, or, if they already lived in an urban setting, they were rehoused in the town planning process, or, in some cases, they moved to a more affluent area of residence as their standard of living improved.

In *The Journey Home* Dermot Bolger[14] analyses the phenomenon of the erosion of traditional values and the transformation of customs and rites in families who have moved from rural or close-knit inner city communities to housing estates on the

145

periphery of Dublin. He describes the gradual change which comes upon the first generation of these uprooted people who only 'half belong', and the more sudden change which affects the second generation. Hano, Dermot Bolger's second generation hero, expresses it thus: 'As long as I remained among the hens and barking dogs [of the Dublin estate where he lived with his Kerry born parents] I too could belong, but each walk home from school by the new shopping arcades, each programme on the television religiously switched on at half-five in every terraced house, was thrusting me out in my own time. I began bringing home phrases that couldn't fit in that house when we still knelt for the family rosary. I hid photographs of rock stars beneath my mattress like pornographic pictures, wrote English soccer players' names on my copybook, feeling I was committing an act of betrayal'.[15] With the referring to the switching on of the television as an activity performed with the regularity of a religious ritual, and the mention of English football players having achieved heroic status in the eyes of the second generation, the two old bulwarks of Irish society, Catholicism and nationalism, are shown to have definitely broken up.

Feminism has also emerged as a force which greatly contributed, and still does, to the transformation of Irish society. By feminism, I mean the general and gradual consciousness of Irish women of the role they could actively play in the shaping of the world they live in; it meant breaking away from the traditional pattern, enshrined in the 1937 Constitution, of the woman as mainly a wife and a mother, shaping only the restricted area of the home. A complexity of factors triggered off this growing awareness: the models coming from abroad through television, magazines and more extensive travelling abroad, not to forget about the impact of Irish (female) emigrants returning home on regular visits; new opportunities for female employment (for instance the growing economic sector of the services) which happened to suit women at a time when they were ready to join the workforce; the removal of some legal barriers which had excluded married women from the civil service;[16] the increasing availability of contraceptives – though extremely restricted at the beginning of the period studied – and the ways found to divert the total ban on the sale and importation of contraceptives prior to 1974.[17] Though feminism as such is not primarily concerned with the Church, the more militant elements of the feminist movement have been quick to point out the male domination pervading the Catholic Church particularly, and the sexist nature of many of its dogmas on the family and sexual morality. Though secularisation is not an issue formulated as such by Irish women, it is nevertheless the pattern which their changing attitudes in key areas has followed.

The two main transformations in women's lives since the 1960s have been their greater access to the workplace and the control that they have exercised over their fertility. The two transformations happened more or less together, the latter facilitating the former. In their analysis of 'State, Class and Family', Richard Breen *et al.* make the following remarks: 'Perhaps the clearest indicator of the extent and suddenness of the change in the Irish family is the labour force participation rate of married women: in 1961, one in twenty was in the workforce; in 1987, one out of every five married women is a labour force participant.'[18] In 1993, the proportion amounted to one in three married women in the labour force.[19] The increasing proportion of married women in the labour force is a clear indication that Irish women are no longer subscribing to the role they were assigned in the constitution, which largely reflected Catholic social teaching on the family.

Women have generally become more independent, planning their lives as they see best and not systematically in reference to a male dominated society and Church. Three factors are revealing of women's emancipation: the use of artificial contraception, the amount of births taking place outside marriage, and the growing number of legal separations being initiated by women. The Catholic Church being still particularly strict on these issues, the changes indicate a definite stance by Irish women: they are no longer subscribing to the Church's teaching on procreation and marriage.

I think the evidence of a widespread practice of contraception among Irish women is revealing of a strong loss of authority on the part of the Catholic Church and of a breaking-off of its traditional alliance with women. In 1968, when the Pope reaffirmed the Church's stance on contraception and spoke against it in his encyclical *Humanae vitae,* many women felt they were being 'let down' by the Church; some of them were already resorting to artificial means of contraception and were hoping that the Church, in the wake of the changes brought about by the Second Vatican Council, would endorse it (Graph 1 clearly shows that the birth-rate had started to decline in the mid-sixties, going down to 21.0 per 1,000 of population in 1968, having reached 22.4 in 1964); others were hoping that they could start once the Church agreed. After *Humanae vitae,* Irish women continued for some time to have large families: the birth-rate remained high until 1973 at 22.4 per 1,000 in that year. But in the mid-seventiess, the birth-rate started to decline: it went down to 22.1 in 1974, and more significantly, it oscillated between 21.0 and 21.2 in the years 1975 to 1978. Then, in the wake of the papal visit to Ireland in September 1979, there was an upsurge of catholicism again for about a year: the birth-rate went up to 21.8 in 1980 (see the peak corresponding to that year on the graph) and many male babies were called John Paul. After that, women resorted to emancipation and took no heed of the Catholic Church's teaching on artificial contraception: the birth-rate has steadily declined since 1981, from 21.0 in 1981 to 13.9 in 1993.

Graph 1
Birth rate 1958-1993 (per 1,000 population)[20]

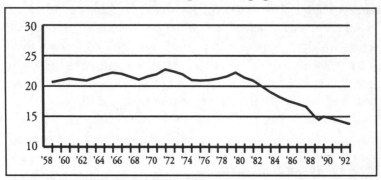

As far as births outside marriage are concerned, the rate was relatively stable and low until 1980 (less than 5 per cent of total births), only reaching over 10 per cent in 1987, and then increasing steadily to reach 19.5 per cent in 1993. Graph 2 clearly shows the evolution.

Graph 2
Births Outside Marriage 1963-1993
(as a Percentage of Total Births)[21]

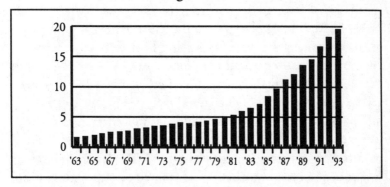

Some of the conclusions of a survey of unmarried mothers who were delivered in the National Maternity Hospital between 1986 and 1988[22] are interesting for our study of secularisation:

there has been a steady increase in the numbers of mothers deciding to parent their children, which would reflect better acceptance of unmarried mothers at societal level and better provision at state level; a considerable number of the mothers were either living with the putative father of the child (16-19 per cent) or were involved in stable relationships at the time of delivery (50 per cent), which would indicate a certain amount of choice in favour of having a child outside the bond of marriage.

The institution of marriage has been taking quite a battering in Ireland in recent times. We have just seen that it is no longer the sole, sacrosanct place for procreation. It has been hit by a decline in the number of marriages and by a sharp increase in marital breakdown.[23] This increase is an indication that people in general no longer look upon the institution of marriage as a lifelong commitment, no matter what the circumstances, according to the Catholic rules, but what is even more relevant is that women have had a far greater tendency than men to register themselves as separated in the surveys and that they have been instrumental in initiating legal separations. In the 1986 and 1991 censuses, as well as in the Labour Force Surveys since 1983, there have been consistently higher numbers of separated women than men, with the Labour Force Surveys in 1986, 1988 and 1989 even registering twice as many women as men who declare themselves to be separated. This inconsistency, already pointed out by Tony Fahey and Maureen Lyons in their study on marital breakdown, 'could reflect the influence of behavioural factors – higher emigration among separated men, or a higher rate of entry into second unions – but it could also reflect a lesser willingness among men to define themselves as separated'.[24] The latter suggestion might be the main explanation, as women's assertiveness in the area of marital breakdown has been shown to exceed that of men in the area of initiating legal resolutions. The conclusion reached by Fahey and Lyons is that 'women are more than

three times more likely to take the initiative in
conflicts to law than are men'.[25]

The fact that women are becoming more and 1
from Catholic teaching on the family and sexua
bound to have huge consequences on the whole fat
society. Women had traditionally been instrumental in   ...d-
ing on of the faith to children, both in inculcating the strict
moral code on sexual matters as defined by the Catholic Church
and also possibly, in arousing vocations. Tom Inglis has developed the theme of the Catholic mother as the key figure in the
church's lay support and he has pointed out that changes in the
position of women in economic life and in the family have led to
changes in the position of the Catholic Church in society as a
whole.[26]

Besides, there is evidence of a growing sense of alienation
among women from the institutional Church. A survey carried
out in 1992 by the Subcommittee on Women in the Church,[27]
among women who considered themselves committed Catholics,
found a high level of anger and hurt. Over two-thirds (68 per
cent) of the respondents felt a sense of anger at the way women
are treated in the Church, while just 11 per cent felt the Church
authorities were supportive of women. A total of 57 per cent felt
hurt by the Church – either by the form of liturgy, by what the
Church says or by the interpretation of scripture. Further analysis of women's religious practice will also prove useful at a later
stage of the study.

The media have played a decisive role in undermining the
Catholic Church's authority in Ireland. The general tone of edi-
torials and of most popular programmes is unequivocally one
advocating liberalism and pluralism. We must differentiate
between the reporting of events directly linked with the institutional Church, the treatment of socio-political issues, and the
staging of soaps on radio and television. It is striking that in a
country with such a strong tradition of Catholicism as Ireland,

...re should be so little 'serious' discussion about the institutional Church; the media consistently either openly launch attacks on the Church or trivialise religious issues. The fact that the media in Ireland seem to overreact where the Church is concerned, is revealing of a society where the weight of the Catholic Church had been excessive. It is a sign that Irish society is still in the throes of trying to come to terms with an excess of Church authority and that it is attempting to find an adjustment. The Church's imposition of strict control in the area of people's morals is still so recent that Irish people, and this is particularly striking among journalists and broadcasters who are in the public eye, are still caught up in a kind of 'revenge logic' and haven't yet been able to progress further. While it was the role of the media to expose publicly the scandals involving religious since 1992, the reports have often been tinted with sensationalism, even in some usually 'serious' newspapers. Trivialisation has also been a way for the media to deal with Church issues, which would indicate either a conscious reduction in the importance of religious issues or a lack of knowledge about religious matters, or both.

When it comes to the treatment of socio-political matters, the media has been both an eye-opener for Irish people and a means of coming to terms with the changes in their society. As early as 1966, television had been introduced into 85 per cent of all Irish homes;[28] it has thus had a considerable impact on a great majority of the population during the last thirty years. The role of chat-shows on the radio and television, and particularly that of the *Late Late Show,* has been recognised as having had an enormous influence; such shows enabled public debate of issues which up to then had either been hushed up or spoken of only in private. Moreover, they enabled ordinary Irish people to discuss vital contemporary issues with other ordinary Irish people.

Now I would like to turn to the portrayal of the Church and of values associated with the Catholic ethos in some popular television programmes. When RTE started producing its own 'soaps' in the mid-sixties, producers experienced a certain number of difficulties in terms of 'how far they could go'. In her book *Irish Television Drama,* Helena Sheehan comments on the restrictions contronting the producer of *The Riordans,* Wesley Burrowes, from the mid-sixties through to the seventies, and how he dealt with them. All incidents except one related to sexual morality and its transgressions. Introducing the issue of unmarried motherhood proved quite difficult: 'There were two attempts to introduce a story-line in which Maggie Nael[29] would become pregnant. Overruled both times, Burrowes sought alternative strategies. The first time the unmarried mother story was introduced via an outsider, an English Protestant one at that, to distance it and to make it less highly charged for an Irish Catholic audience'.[30] Introducing the issue of extra-marital sex proved equally difficult: '(…) after Benjy and Maggie had married (…) Benjy's eyes (and a bit more than his eyes) began to wander. An attempt to explore the effects of an extra-marital affair on a marital relationship resulted in the scripts being gutted'.[31] In the 1990s Roddy Doyle experienced no difficulty whatsoever in his serial *Family,* transmitted in May 1994, when he portrayed marital infidelity and breakdown in very explicit images; by then, both issues had been debated widely in Irish society and it was widely accepted that such problems existed in its midst.

The time is long gone in Irish soap operas since the priest had an influence on the way people lead their private lives. In *The Riordans,* the issue of contraception involved the priest, Father Sheehy, to whom Maggie went for advice. Today, the issue of contraception is outdated and not even mentioned in soaps; and it seems that running to the priest for advice on one's private life is just as outdated, that is when the programme features a priest to run to. In *Glenroe,* the parish priest, Father Devereux, has abandoned his vocation. His replacement hasn't featured in the programme, and the older folk in the town are slowly coming to terms with not calling him 'Father' any longer; now, the scenes portraying Father Devereux focus on his attempts to earn a living by fixing old pianos.

Series portraying Irish society today rarely have space for the priest; in Roddy Doyle's *Family*, there was very little mention of religion. The school, the hospital and the pub featured in the programme, but the church was invisible, non-existent. Instead of turning to the parish priest for advice and consolation – he didn't feature in the programme anyway – the mother turned to neighbours, friends and extended family. However, there was one interesting detail which would indicate that religion is not yet completely gone from Ireland's cultural landscape. The mother, having separated from her husband and in the process of finding a new balance in her life, unexpectedly asks her son to say grace before the family meal; his reaction, at first, is one of shock, but prodded by his mother, the forgotten words slowly come back to him. In her distress, the mother still instinctively feels that the ritual of prayer might bring about a sense of peace in the broken family life; it symbolises to some extent the family reconstituted. Incidentally, the son, having been born during the year following the papal visit, is called John Paul. The residues of faith are still there, in this urbanised setting where petty crime is rampant.

There has been a move from concerns centered primarily on the private world to wider issues of social justice. Though concerns centering on individual lives still prevail, all the current 'hype' in *Glenroe* is about a rape trial; in *Fair City*, the issue of the sale of a pizzeria and the fate awaiting the workers faced with the prospect of unemployment, has come up recently. The fact that the focus has moved away from the family and sexual morality would indicate that these issues have more or less been come to terms with and that society is now focusing on others. The strict moral code imposed by the Catholic Church in these areas is no longer relevant and Irish people have attained a certain level of maturity in being able to decide for themselves.

Towards a new pattern in religious practice?

A more thorough investigation of the process of secularisation would require that religious beliefs and moral values be also taken into consideration; however, given the limitations of this publication, I will deal only with the changes which have affected religious practice.

First, a brief mention of religious affiliation is interesting. The striking feature over the period studied concerns the increase in the number of people who have declared themselves as having 'no religion' in the censuses of population and in a survey carried out by Lansdowne Market Research in March 1994.[32] In the 1961 census, the category hardly existed, at 0.039 per cent of the population; in the 1991 census, it had increased to 1.88 per cent, but the most significant increase was registered in the 1994 survey, with 5 per cent of people in the sample declaring to have no religion. In other words, the number of people declaring themselves as having no religion was multiplied by 48 between 1961 and 1991, by 2.66 between 1991 and 1994, and by 128 between 1961 and 1994. This could be explained both by the fact that a proportion of the population has become estranged from religion over that thirty-year period and also by the fact that in the 1990s, Irish people can be more open about their religious affiliation, in comparison to the early 1960s. However, overall, at the end of the twentieth century, Ireland still registers an extremely high proportion of the population belonging to a denomination. In Europe, it shares with Portugal the highest proportion of Catholics: 91 per cent.[33] Having said this, it must be stressed that raw census figures and the measure of religious affiliation itself might not mean much, as a large proportion of the people who have a sense of belonging to a religion can in fact call themselves Catholic or whatever else, without being actually involved in the practice and beliefs of that faith. In some cases, people would have lost all commitment to and contact with the institutional Church.

High levels of religious practice have been characteristic of Irish Catholics. In the first chapter of his major work on the relations between Church and state in Ireland from 1923 to 1979, John Whyte remarks: 'Ireland is unusual in having a large majority, not just of Catholics, but of committed and practising Catholics'.[34] This remark, however, is already seventeen years old at the time of writing. What we need to assess is the level of commitment as it stands in 1996 or as close to it as statistics will allow.

The survey on religious attitudes and beliefs carried out by Dr Máire Nic Ghiolla Phádraig[35] for the Irish hierarchy in 1973/74 registered for the first time that a significant minority was not attending Mass weekly and had abandoned the practice of annual reception of the sacraments; it involved 25 per cent of single males and females aged between eighteen and thirty, and 30 per cent of single males and females aged between twenty-one and twenty-five. There have been various surveys on religious practice since then – Table 1 and Graph 3 show the evolution from 1973 to 1995, according to Mass attendance figures available from nine surveys.

Table 1
Weekly (or more frequent) Mass Attendance 1973-1995

Year Data Collected	Mass Attendance (%)	Source
1973-74	90.9	*A Survey of Religious Practice, Attitudes and Beliefs 1973-74,* M. Nic Ghiolla Phádraig, Maynooth: Council for Research and Development, 1975.
1981	87	*Irish Values and Attitudes: The Irish Report of the European Value Systems Study,* Michael Fogarty, Joseph Lee and Liam Ryan, 1984.

1983	86.9	*Religious Beliefs, Practice and Moral Attitudes: A Comparison of Two Irish Surveys 1974-84,* Ann Breslin and John Weafer, Maynooth: Council for Research and Development, 1985.
1988-89	81.6	*Religious Practice and Attitudes in Ireland 1988-89,* Micheál Mac Gréil, Maynooth: St Patrick's College, Department of Social Studies, 1991.
1990	85	*Values and Social Change in Ireland,* C. Whelan (ed.), Dublin: Gill & Macmillan, 1994, p.21.
1992	78	'A Church in Recession – Three National Surveys, 1974-1992', John Weafer, Maynooth: *The Furrow,* April 1993, vol. 44, no.4.
1994	77	'Mass Attendance', Omnibus Research, Lansdowne Market Research, March 1994.

(Attendance at religious services[36])

1995	76	*Standard Eurobarometer* 42, Eurostat, Luxembourg, July 1995, p.76.

1995	64	IMS national poll, *Sunday Independent/ Late Late Show,* October 1995.

Graph 3
Weekly (or more) Mass attendance 1973-1995

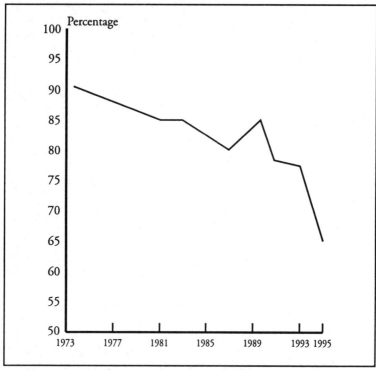

From 1973/74 to 1988/89, that is in fifteen years, the decline in the rate of Mass attendance was equal to 10.2 per cent; between 1992 and 1995, the rate declined by 18 per cent; between 1994 and 1995, it declined by 17 per cent. In other words, the picture was one of relative stability until 1990, with levels of Mass attendance over 80 per cent, but the latest poll registers a dramatic decrease in the nineteen months separating the last two surveys.

It is interesting here to compare the Irish situation with that of its European Union partners. Compared with the other members of the EU, Ireland still has by far the highest weekly attendance at religious services: 25 per cent of the EU population say

they attend religious services once or more often per week, concentrated in Ireland (76 per cent according to *Eurobarometer* 42
in July 1995, but we must remember that the most recent survey
gave a figure of 64 per cent), Italy (42 per cent), Portugal (37 per
cent) and Spain (35 per cent).[37]

The frequency of attending religious services gives further
indications. The following table gives the frequency of Mass
attendance over twenty two years; the first two dates correspond
to the two major reports on religious practice done at a ten-year
interval, the last three correspond to the latest surveys.

Table 2
Frequency of Mass Attendance 1973-1995 (%)

	1974	1984	1992	1994	1995
Once a week (or more)	91	87	78	77	64
At least once a month	3	4	7	7	11
Less than once a month	3	6	11	11	17
Never	3	3	3	5	8

The proportion of Irish people who never go to Mass, very
low and stable until 1992, registered a slight increase in 1994,
which was confirmed by a further increase in 1995: it now concerns 8 per cent of the population. This proportion remains
below the proportion of EU citizens who claim they never attend
religious services: 13 per cent of the EU population, the highest
being 21 per cent in France.[38] However, the figure is getting closer to the European average and would seem to indicate that Irish
people's religious practice is converging towards that of other
Europeans.

Besides, the trend which Table 2 above registers is that of a more irregular attendance; if we take the two categories 'at least once a month' and 'less than once a month', that is less than the minimum required by the Catholic Church, we obtain the following trend: 1974 (6 per cent), 1984 (10 per cent), 1992 (18 per cent), 1994 (18 per cent), 1995 (28 per cent). The proportion of 'irregular Mass-goers' has significantly increased by 10 per cent in the nineteen months separating the last two surveys. If we add the proportion of those who never attend, we obtain the following assessment: 36 per cent of Irish people either attend Mass irregularly or never, that is more than a third of the total population. Compared to the other EU members, the proportion of Irish people who are irregular Mass attenders is still well below average. Thirty-eight per cent of EU citizens claim to attend – religious services, as opposed to strictly Mass – 'a few times a year': 64 per cent in Greece, 49 per cent in Denmark and 43 per cent in the Netherlands; one in five EU citizens claim to attend religious services 'once a year or less' (32 per cent of the French attend once a year or less).[39]

I think special attention should be given to Saturday evening Mass attendance as opposed to Sunday morning since, traditionally, Sunday has been a day devoted to the act of worship. In the 1994 Lansdowne Market Research survey, although the majority of respondents (59 per cent) continue to attend Mass on Sunday mornings and 4 per cent attend on Sunday evening, a significant proportion (34 per cent) attend Saturday evening Mass. I think the shift from attending mass on Sunday to Saturday is a sign of secularisation on the part both of the laity and of the Church. Besides, the increasing status of Sunday as a day of trading in recent years in Ireland is significant; it is of particular significance that at Christmas time especially, shops should be open on Sundays. It is a clear example of consumerism having superseded the most Christian occasion of the year.

Besides Mass attendance, two sacramental practices should be taken into account when trying to assess the extent and the evolution of religious practice: they are the sacraments of communion and confession. Table 3, a combination of Micheál Mac Gréil's report on religious attitudes and practice in the Republic of Ireland in 1988/89 and of the latest survey done by the IMS in October 1995, shows the developments from 1973 to 1995.

Table 3
Frequency of Sacramental Practice of Roman Catholics
1973-74, 1984, 1988-89, and 1995 (%)

	1974	1984	1988-9	1995	Differences			
	A	B	C	D	A-B (10 yrs)	B-C (5 yrs)	C-D (6 yrs)	A-D (21 yrs)
Weekly Mass Attendance	91	87	82	64	-4	-5	-18	-27
Weekly Holy Communion	28	38	43	39	+10	+5	-4	+11
Monthly Confessions	47	26	18	14	-21	-8	-4	-33

The graphs corresponding to the evolution of weekly Holy Communion and monthly confessions from 1973 to 1995 give us a visual idea of this evolution:

Graph 4
Weekly Holy Communion 1973-1995

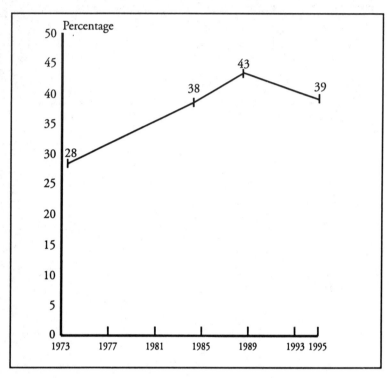

Graph 5
Monthly Confessions 1973-1995

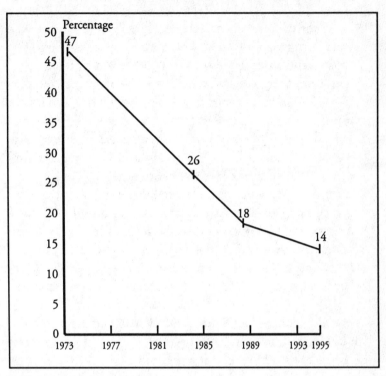

Two factors should be noted here:
- There was a very substantial increase in the frequency of weekly reception of Holy Communion between 1973/74 and 1988/89 (1 per cent per annum), which clearly indicates a change in the level of participation of those going to Mass. The extent of the increase (15 per cent) is significantly higher than the decline in weekly Mass attendance (-9 per cent) over the fifteen years from 1974 to 1989, which indicates that there was a change from a monolithic Catholic block who practised on a large scale to a congregation which had become more selective: Catholics were either beginning to

163

drift away from religion altogether or, when they still practised, they became more involved. However, the decline registered in the practice of Holy Communion in 1995 is a
cause for concern: it indicates that it is not just those who
were marginally attached who are dropping out, but that
there is also a decline in the most committed section.

- There has been a dramatic decline in the frequency of going
  to confession at least monthly. It clearly indicates a change of
  norm among Catholics in Ireland, as the practice of sacramental confessions had been a strong characteristic of Irish
  Roman Catholicism. I would like to add one remark concerning the dramatic decline in attending confessions: the
  increase in 'chat-shows' on the radio and television, and the
  proliferation of associations and groups, in aid of various
  causes and offering support in the form of individual counselling and group discussions, have greatly reduced the need
  for people to go to a priest for exposing their personal problems and finding some sort of understanding and comfort.

In order to assess more precisely how religious practice varies
with modernisation, it is necessary to take a number of variables
into consideration.[40] I will not enter into any details here as Dr
Christopher Whelan and Dr Tony Fahey have done extensive
research in this area,[41] including a paper presented at this symposium on 'Religion and Social Change in Ireland'. I will only
briefly mention one of the four variables – the effect of gender –
as I made the point that women's changing roles were a major
agent in the secularisation of Irish society.

Women have traditionally been more religious than men,
attending Mass more frequently, going to communion and confession more regularly. However, there is evidence that, as women
join the labour force, they practise their faith less and their level
of religiosity converges towards that of men. According to the
1990 European Values Survey, 93 per cent of women who work

full-time in the home attend Mass weekly as opposed to 78 per cent of those who are in full-time employment outside the home. This indicates convergence towards the figure for men in full-time employment (75 per cent).[42] The traditionally higher level of religiosity among women is thus evidently vanishing with the increase in women working outside the home. Broadly speaking, in the 1973/74 and 1984 surveys on religious practice, gender was a significant factor; but by the late 1980s, the gender gap had vanished concerning Mass attendance. However, women were still twice as likely (50 per cent) to receive Holy Communion as men (27 per cent) in 1995,[43] which indicates there is still a gender gap in relation to the practice of communion.

The impact of the scandals in the Church

The study of religious practice has shown a sharp decline in the 1990s, and particularly between the last two surveys done in 1994 and 1995. Besides the general ongoing modernisation process of Irish society in the 1990s, a series of sex scandals involving Church members has been brought to the attention of the public by the media. It seems inevitable and undeniable that these revelations have deeply affected the Catholic community, particularly when the Irish Church had placed so much emphasis on obedience to the Catholic moral code in matters pertaining to sexuality and the family.

The Bishop Casey affair in 1992, followed by the Brendan Smyth affair in 1994, the ensuing series of paedophile priests cases and the revelations of children's neglect in orphanages run by nuns, have highlighted the discrepancy between what the clergy teach and what they do; if Catholics could come to terms with accepting that the clergy numbered a small minority of deviants, they found it much more difficult to accept the mishandling of these cases by the hierarchy. In a world where public accountability matters more and more, the lack of an adequate response by the Church could prove fatal.

Once people become estranged from the institutional Church and learn how to lead their lives without the help of religion and its codes, it is very unlikely they will drift back in again. Because Irish Catholicism had always placed a strong emphasis on legalism, there is a great danger that when the authority of the Church is undermined, the formerly high levels of religious adherence will collapse. However, it would seem that Irish people so far have mainly shown signs of changing attitudes towards the clergy and decreasing trust in the institutional Church rather than loss of faith as such.

The findings of a survey of attitudes to the Catholic Church carried out in January 1995 are helpful, as are those of the IMS poll done in November 1995. The first survey was commissioned by RTÉ's *Would you Believe* programme and carried out by Lansdowne Market Research. The primary purpose of the survey was to 'assess the extent to which confidence in and respect for the Catholic Church has been undermined by recent media exposure of sexual abuse of children by some members of the clergy'. On the issue of the implications of revelations about Father Brendan Smyth, 42 per cent of Catholics interviewed claim that they have less respect for the Catholic Church, whereas only 17 per cent feel a loss of their own personal faith (with only 4 per cent having lost 'a lot of faith' as compared to 13 per cent who had only lost 'a little faith'). This difference between the high level of decline in respect for the Church on the one hand, and the low level of loss of personal faith on the other, corroborates the suggestion that Irish people are becoming estranged from the institutional Church, but remain largely close to their faith. In the IMS poll, the number of Catholics who feel that the Catholic Church has been permanently damaged by the scandals about paedophile priests has grown to 57 per cent (this question could be equated with the one in the previous survey on the loss of respect for the Church). The sharp division between the generations on the issue also proves extremely revealing: while just

44 per cent of those aged sixty-five agreed, 75 per cent of those under thirty-four said yes to that question. In the short period of time between the two surveys (only ten months), the increase in the lack of respect for the Church – all ages merged – has been very steep. A follow-up question on the issue of the damage done to the Catholic Church by scandals about priests and child sexual abuse asked: 'Because of these scandals has your own level of trust in the Church decreased?' Forty-one per cent of respondents answered 'yes', which is very high. It was mentioned that the greatest loss of confidence was amongst the young but it didn't give any breakdown of figures. Interestingly, more women (44 per cent) than men (38 per cent) said their trust had diminished.

Unfortunately, the question concerning the loss of personal faith wasn't asked in the IMS poll, so the comparison with the earlier survey proves more difficult on this issue. However, the journalist who reported the findings of the IMS poll did mention that respondents were asked whether their basic religious beliefs were shaken by these events; the results given were that opinion was split evenly on that question and that, once again, women (52 per cent) were slightly more likely than men (46 per cent) to have been affected. The question was not as clear as the one on the extent of loss of faith in the previous survey, but it still remains that the percentage of the respondents saying that their basic religious beliefs have been shaken (50 per cent) is very high indeed, and indicates that the spate of child sexual abuse by priests and religious revealed in the course of 1995 has triggered off both a loss of trust in the institutional Church and a loss of personal faith. Given the January 1995 survey results, it seems that the Bishop Casey and Brendan Smyth affairs had mainly shaken Catholics' trust in the Church as an institution but not as a body of beliefs. However, it seems that the accumulation of scandals and above all the poor handling of the cases by the hierarchy, ranging from the mere transfer of culprits from one parish to another, to the huge sums of money paid to victims in order to buy their silence, to the general reluctance and inability to deal with the grave matters promptly and efficiently once they were uncovered, have proven too much for many Irish Catholics to accept.

Overall, what remains more striking is the changing attitude towards the clergy. I think the controversy which followed Bishop Comiskey's return to his diocese also shows that Irish people have less trust in the hierarchy, but it doesn't follow suit that they are abandoning their faith. Many people want him to answer questions on his handling of sex abuse cases in his diocese, which is revealing of the fact that the Church's authority is being challenged by the faithful; it is a sign that the Church is being considered as another power force in society and not as a superior authoritarian force which isn't to be challenged. Some of the people in Wexford have even said that he should resign, that they didn't want him to confirm their children, thus expressing a 'vote of no confidence' in him. However, it hasn't been reported that, as a result of the whole affair, some Wexford people were considering not having their children confirmed at all. The faithful are not giving up on the ritual and sacraments of the Church, they just want its representatives to be accountable.

To conclude, I think it is possible to say that the 1960s was a period when the factors which were to bring about secularisation were put in place. In the 1970s, Irish people and, more strikingly, women, started changing their habits – particularly in the area of private morality – which so far had been very much influenced by Catholic dogma; the first decline in religious practice was registered. In the 1980s, further changes were registered – women's control over their fertility became a well-established practice, for instance – but generally speaking the picture remained one of relative stability. With the 1990s however, a marked increase in the drift from religion, and particularly from the institutional Church, has come.

However, change is cohabiting with continuity. While religious practice is getting closer to European norms, secularisation in Ireland is taking place at a slower pace than had been expected, considering its level of modernisation, and has remained much more insulated from secularising influences than its western counterparts. While the study of the impact of the scandals involving religious has shown that Irish people have less trust in the institutional Church, it has also shown that they generally still hold on to their personal faith. While the alienation of women is a notable phenomenon and one which has repercussions on the whole fabric of society, there has been renewed interest in theology on the part of women particularly. In an article published in *The Irish Times* on 3 January 1996 Dr Enda McDonagh remarked: 'Irish theology … is currently enjoying new energy, freedom and variety with the influx of lay students, particularly women students, both young and mature. In a decade or so the best and most creative theologians in Ireland and in many other places will be lay and probably women. The varieties of Irish Catholicism will be the richer for it.'

NOTES

1. E. Larkin, 'The devotional revolution in Ireland, 1850-1875', in *Historical Dimensions of Irish Catholicism*, New York, Arno, 1976.
2. *Monarchie absolue de droit divin.*
3. The Campaign to Separate Church and State is the only militant organisation involved in the laicisation of institutions I am aware of, but it doesn't have national widespread influence; it has a relatively low membership, and the extent of its support would be quite small.
4. R. Nisbet, *The Social Bond*, New York, Knopf, 1970.
5. M. Hornsby-Smith, 'Social and Religious Transformations in Ireland: A Case of Secularisation?', in *The Development of Industrial Society in Ireland*, John Goldthorpe and Christopher Whelan (eds.), Oxford, Oxford University Press, 1992, p. 289.

6. A. M. Greeley, *The Persistence of Religion,* London, SCM Press Ltd, 1973, p. 14.
7. M. Nic Ghiolla Phádraig, 'Ireland: The Exception That Proves Two Rules', in *World Catholicism in Transition,* T. Gannon (ed.), London, Macmillan, 1988, p. 206.
8. This example was given by Professor Maurice Goldring, who lectures in Irish Studies at the University of Paris VIII, in a paper read at a symposium held in the Irish College in Paris in May 1992 on the theme 'Ireland: Towards a Secular Society?' His paper, as yet unpublished, was entitled 'Sécularisation'.
9. In French, the word *siècle* which translates into century, means both a period of a hundred years, and life in 'the world', as opposed to religious life. The term 'secular' translates in French into *séculier,* that is, which belongs to the 'siècle', to the life of the laity, as opposed to the life of the religious, or to the members of the clergy who live in 'the world' as opposed to those in religious orders who live apart.
10. Larkin, op. cit., p. 636.
11. New objectives of national economic policy launched by T. K. Whitaker, Secretary of the Department of Finance.
12. Statistical Abstract 1994, Central Statistics Office, p. 52.
13. C. Whelan (ed.), *Values and Social Change in Ireland,* Dublin, Gill & Macmillan, 1994, p. 15.
14. D. Bolger, *The Journey Home,* London, Penguin Books, 1991.
15. Bolger, op. cit., p. 7.
16. The ban on married women working in the civil service was removed in 1973 when Ireland joined the EEC.
17. The 1935 Criminal Law Amendment Act forbade the sale and importation of contraceptives. However, a significant number of Irish women – with the help of some doctors – found ways to get around the law. When the pill became available in Ireland in the mid-sixties, an incredible number

of Irish women seem to have suffered menstrual irregularities, as the pill could only be prescribed as a cycle regulator. When the first family planning services were set up in 1969 on a voluntary basis, contraceptives were not sold but exchanged for a donation. In 1973/74, the famous McGee case opened the door to the liberalisation of contraception, with the Supreme Court ordering the state to remove the ban on the importation of contraceptives for personal use.

18. R. Breen, D. Hannan, D. Rottman and C. Whelan, *Understanding Contemporary Ireland; State, Class and Development in the Republic of Ireland,* Dublin, Gill & Macmillan, 1990, p. 101.

19. Statistic compiled from figures available in the Labour Force Survey, 1993, Central Statistics Office.

20. Health Statistics, 1992, Department of Health, and Vital Statistics, First Quarter 1994, Department of Health.

21. Statistical Abstracts, 1970-71, 1976, 1982-85 and Statistical Bulletin, 1994, Central Statistics Office.

22. J. Donohoe, A. Fitzpatrick, N. Flanagan and S. Scanlan, *Unmarried Mothers delivered in the National Maternity Hospital 1988,* Dublin, National Maternity Hospital/UCD, 1990.

23. It must, however, be borne in mind that, placed in an international context of developed countries, Ireland has a much lower rate of marital breakdown than the high divorce countries, and ranks similar to the low divorce countries, with the separated in Ireland, according to 1991 census data, amounting to just under 4 per cent of the ever-married population.

24. T. Fahey and Maureen Lyons, *Marital Breakdown and Family Law in Ireland, A Sociological Study,* Dublin, ESRI, 1995, p. 100.

25. Fahey and Lyons, op. cit., p. 66.

26. T. Inglis, *Moral Monopoly, The Catholic Church in Modern Irish Society,* Dublin, Gill & Macmillan, 1987, chapter 8, pp. 187-214.

27. *Women in the Church in Ireland,* Dublin, Irish Commission for Justice and Peace, 1993.
28. Helena Sheehan, *Irish Television Drama, A Society and its Stories,* Dublin, RTE, 1987, p. 138.
29. That is, when she was single, before her marriage to Benjy.
30. Sheehan, op. cit., p. 159.
31. Sheehan, op. cit., p. 159.
32. Omnibus Research, Lansdowne Market Research Limited, March 1994.
33. *Standard Eurobarometer* 42, Eurostat, Luxembourg, July 1995, p. 76.
34. J. Whyte, *Church and State in Modern Ireland 1923-1979,* Dublin, Gill & Macmillan, 1980, p. 4.
35. M. Nic Ghiolla Phádraig, *A Survey of Religious Practice, Attitudes and Beliefs 1973-1974,* PhD thesis, UCD, 1981.
36. The question asked in *Standard Eurobarometer* 42 focused on attendance at religious services rather than on Mass attendance only.
37. *Standard Eurobarometer* 42, op. cit., p. 76.
38. *Standard Eurobarometer* 42, op. cit., p. 77.
39. *Standard Eurobarometer* 42, op. cit., p. 77.
40. Four variables can be regarded as indicators of the modernisation process: gender, age, occupational status/education, and area of residence.
41. Their research can be found in Whelan, op. cit.
42. Whelan, op. cit., p. 24.
43. IMS poll, *Sunday Independent,* 5 November 1995.

BIOGRAPHICAL NOTES
ON THE CONTRIBUTORS

Most Rev Donal Murray DD is Bishop of Limerick. He lectured in Moral Theology in the Mater Dei Institute of Education and in Holy Cross College, Clonliffe from 1969 to 1982. From 1982 until 1996 he was an Auxiliary Bishop of Dublin. He is a member of the Pontifical Council for Culture.

Rev Fachtna McCarthy STL lectures in theology at St Patrick's College of Education, Drumcondra. He studied in Rome at the Lateran and Gregorian Universities and at Notre Dame, Indiana. With his colleague Fr Joseph McCann CM he recently won a prestigious award from the Templeton Foundation for the Promotion of Dialogue between Science and Religion.

Rev Eoin G. Cassidy DPh is a lecturer in Philosophy at the Mater Dei Institute of Education in Dublin. He obtained his doctorate in Philosophy in 1990 from the Institut Supérieur de Philosophie, Louvain, Belgium. He is a former treasurer of the Irish Philosophy Society and secretary of the Irish Theological Society.

Rev Michael Paul Gallagher SJ, PhD, after university studies in Dublin, France, Oxford and the United States, became a lecturer in Modern English and American Literature in University College, Dublin, where he taught from 1972 to 1990. From 1990 to 1995 he worked in the Pontifical Council for Culture in the Vatican, and now divides his life between teaching fundamental theology at the Gregorian University, Rome, and various ministries in Ireland. His most recent books are *What are they saying about Unbelief?* (Paulist, 1995) and *Questions of Faith* (Veritas, 1996). A few months after the publication of this volume his *Chasing Symbols,* dealing with faith and culture, will be published (Darton, Longman & Todd).

Rev Michael Drumm STL is a lecturer in Systematic Theology at the Mater Dei Institute of Education. He has lectured widely on adult religious education programmes throughout Ireland and is currently engaged in research on the effects of the Great Hunger on the religious consciousness of Irish Catholics.

Marguerite Corish MA is a graduate of the Sorbonne in Paris. She is currently researching for a PhD on the secularisation of Irish society for the University of Caen in Normandy. She takes a lectureship in the English department of the University of Lyon in October 1996.

Christopher T. Whelan PhD is a Research Professor in the Economic and Social Research Institute, Dublin. He has written extensively on a range of social issues, especially social mobility and the causes and consequences of unemployment and poverty. He edited and was the main author of a volume based on the 1990 European Values Survey entitled *Values and Social Change in Ireland* (Gill & Macmillan, 1994).

Tony Fahey PhD is a Senior Research Officer in the Economic and Social Research Institute, Dublin. His current research centres mainly on the family and demography, but he has also written on religion in Ireland, with special reference to the development of Catholicism in Ireland since the late nineteenth century.

Joseph Dunne PhD lectures in philosophy in the Education and Human Development programmes in St Patrick's College, Drumcondra. He has spoken and published extensively in

Ireland and abroad on philosophical and educational issued. Dr Dunne is author of *Back to the Rough Ground: 'Phronesis' and 'Techne' in Modern Philosophy and in Aristotle* (University of Notre Dame Press, 1993).